D1297385

WOMEN IN PROTEST 1800 – 1850

Women in Protest, 1800-1850

MALCOLM I. THOMIS AND JENNIFER GRIMMETT

CROOM HELM
London & Canberra

© 1982 Malcolm I. Thomis and Jennifer Grimmett
Croom Helm Ltd, 2 – 10 St John's Road, London SW11

British Library Cataloguing in Publication Data

Thomis, Malcolm I.
  Women in Protest 1800 – 1850.
  1. Social movements — Great Britain — History
  2. Women — Great Britain — History
  I. Title   II. Grimmett, Jennifer
  303.6'0941   HN49.W6
ISBN 0-7099-2407-0

Phototypesetting by Pat Murphy
296b Lymington Road, Highcliffe-on-Sea, Dorset

Printed and bound in Great Britain
by Billing and Sons Limited
Guildford, London, Oxford, Worcester

CONTENTS

ACKNOWLEDGEMENTS

We should like to thank two colleagues from the University of Queensland History Department, Mavis Little, who typed the manuscript, and Mary Kooyman, who helped us to assemble and check material.

For Josephine, already a woman in protest

1 WOMEN'S WORK AND WOMEN'S PROTEST, 1800 – 1850

Women have never held such professional interest for historians as they have in recent years. Since history was first written men have almost monopolised the attention of historians, and this has inevitably left many gaps to be filled and certain sensitivities amongst those whose predecessors have been so badly neglected. It is not the purpose of this text to help to correct the injustices that have been perpetrated by historians and others over the centuries; nor is it the intention to create some theoretical framework within which aspects of women's history can be studied. Its main purpose is simply to suggest that in the area of social and political protest women of nineteenth-century Britain might well have had a significant role that has not yet been fully described and explained; if this is so, then here is a matter worthy of investigation. Full descriptions, let alone full explanations, are still premature, for reasons which will be explained, but partial ones should at least facilitate the task of those who will eventually impose order and meaning upon this little-known subject.

It is possible that most prominent writers on the question of social protest have not said as much about women as their role warrants. If an incomplete account of the past has resulted this is to be regretted, for its own sake and not primarily because it has done an injustice to women. If historians who have looked at this issue are to be criticised for their deficiencies, these must be identified in terms of conclusions which do not follow from the evidence they have examined or of the incompleteness of their evidence; they must not be condemned because women have emerged from their writings with less glory than some people suppose is their due.

The two leading historians of British social protest, George Rudé and Edward Thompson, are both vulnerable to criticism for their treatment of the role of women. Rudé's recent work on 'Protest and Punishment' suggests that out of 3,600 convicts transported for social protest only 120, or 1 in 30, were women and that all but two of these belonged to his fringe group of 'marginal protestors', who were mainly Irish arsonists.[1] His index of 572 identified protestors contains only 4 named women; though 1 in 30 of the total was a woman, only 1 in 143 has been identified and given a specific mention. These figures give rise to such speculation as to the apparently very minor role that women played in protest, the possible partiality of the law in dealing with them, or the possible partiality of the historian in his treatment of them. The English female arsonists sent to Van Diemen's Land, 1840–1853, were 46 in number, but they receive no discussion, and even the intriguing possibility that arson is revealed as the characteristic form of women's protest is undermined by the explanation that the female arsonists were largely intent upon joining their husbands, lovers and brothers in Australia. Food riots, for long associated with women's protest, evidently failed to produce convicts, though transportation sentences were occasionally handed out for food rioting; and Rudé's earlier discussions of food rioting identified socio-economic, rather than gender, groups and associated women's participation with France rather than Britain, despite the known higher incidence of the price-fixing 'taxation populaire' in England.[2] It could safely be concluded that British women play no prominent role in George Rudé's account and explanation of social protest.

Edward Thompson, on his own claim the attempted rescuer of failed minorities (who, by no stretch of the imagination, could be said to include women) from the condescension of posterity, has been berated for treating 'female radicalism with untypical circumspection' and ascribing to women the role of moral supporters of their more active men.[3] This is somewhat surprising criticism of the historian who produced the classic statement on eighteenth-century food rioting in 'The Moral Economy of the English Crowd in the Eighteenth Century', which demonstrated how and why women played a particularly prominent role in food riots.[4] Perhaps the offence of commission there was greater than the earlier one of omission, for it helped to reinforce the image of the stereotype, concerned with matters domestic, especially food prices, and placed women firmly in the market-place, if not exactly beside the kitchen sink. There is evidently a greatly felt need to establish that women's presence in the market-place concerned pamphlets and politics as well as prices, and a more complete account is now being sought.

Setting the limits of an enquiry is not easy, especially with a topic such as social protest, which some would wish to embrace all forms of crime that arise from the failure of society to make proper provision for its members. This study is not concerned with acts of personal gain but with collective action, peaceful and violent, for the achievement of social and political ends carried out usually within what are known as 'popular movements'. Protest will be interpreted broadly to include those actions, often crimes in the law of the times, to change the *status quo* in politics and in industry; although such movements as parliamentary reform and trade unionism were later to become the epitome of constitutional behaviour, they originated none the less in discontent and protest in the period under consideration.

Any attempt to establish the significance of women's role in popular protest must beware of fulfilling its own prophecy that there is a particular role to be identified. It has been suggested, for instance, that whilst their part can be described and even given an emphasis that has previously been lacking, it would be a mistake to suppose that theirs was different and separate from that of males in protest. Their activity, it is said, went well beyond the familiar issue of bread rioting and into matters of greater political content, in the same way that male protest extended over a wide range of subjects and for much the same reasons.[5] It is desirable to know how much women contribute towards 'the changing face of protest' during the first half of the nineteenth century, whether generalisations that have been made about primitive forms of protest, such as food rioting, being superseded by more sophisticated and mature forms, such as political organisation, are true for women in particular;[6] whether women whose involvement in Welsh corn riots in 1793 – 1801 has been explained in terms of their concern with matters affecting the daily lives of the people broadened their concern to include matters of long-term interest such as the acquisition of political power for the remedy of social ills;[7] whether the vision changed as well as the tactics.

The part of it that remained fairly constant was the continued readiness of most women to see politics as a man's world. When women mobilised support for Chartism, they did so, it has been suggested, in support of working-class interests rather than to raise questions related to women,[8] and they were supported in their political activities by men because they were perfectly happy to perpetuate the *status quo* between the sexes. When men felt them-selves threatened, as they sometimes did over jobs and wages, they for their part reacted as men and not as workers and thereby allowed their concern for the primacy of their sex to undermine working-class solidarity over issues on which, it is alleged, they would have been better served by adopting a class position.[9]

Another perspective is that offered by R. S. Neale, who suggests that women were as a whole so restricted in their employment opportunities, so badly paid, so scattered in their places of work, and possessed such an ingrained subjection to authority that they were unable to emerge as a political class. Like the rest of the unskilled they found that their interests as wage earners were not served by working-class organisations and they found it difficult to believe that their interests were those of the working-class movement in general.[10] This view is not in conflict with the findings of John Foster in Oldham that the leadership of the labour movement, which generated class consciousness, contained not one single woman.[11] This seems a more scholarly and empirically based conclusion than the somewhat romantic view that 'recent historical research has documented working women's early and widespread involvement in the class struggle' and the demand to drop the charge that 'nineteenth century working class women were apathetic regarding class action'.[12] Their role in social and political protest can be described; their contribution to the class struggle is a matter of judgement.

If indeed there is no such thing as a specifically female kind of protest, it may be that there is a women's perspective to be observed on particular issues, perhaps a women's slightly different approach to the tactics to be employed in staging a campaign. At all events, it is important to attempt to consider how far women's behaviour in social protest, bread rioting, industrial action or political activity, derives from the fact that participants were involved as women and not simply as people.

In so doing it seems hardly necessary to state that the world of the first half of the nineteenth century was a man's world. The practical consequences of this for a study of women's protest are many. It means for a start that almost all the sources for study are those prepared or collected by men. Not only did men alone speak in Parliament, pass laws and govern, centrally and locally; they also owned and wrote the newspapers of the day, signed requisitions for public meetings, wrote letters to the Home Secretary in their roles as magistrates, mill owners, or in some private capacity. They controlled the content of the material that has been handed down for study and the manner in which it was compiled and presented. Their assumptions about women and their place were fundamental to the way they behaved and expressed themselves, and have, of course, influenced the record as it was compiled.

The terminology of source material presents some problems. It can be taken for granted that almost everyone who used the term universal suffrage meant manhood suffrage, and the unsatisfactory nature of the former term occasionally elicited hostile comments from those who knew that women were not intended and believed they should be. On the other side were those who suggested that women must be comprehended within the term and believed that this made the whole concept a ludicrous one.[13] Descriptions of crowds often cause confusion. The commonly encountered claim that crowds contained large numbers of women and children might mean what it says, but confidence in its literal truth is shaken by the knowledge that writers who sought to play down the size or importance of a gathering chose to do so by alleging that women featured prominently. Reports of women's presence can be cases of accurate reporting or simply disparaging comment. When a report claims that there were large numbers of females at a public execution who would have been better at home attending to their domestic duties, the attitudes of the writer are quite explicit and his reporting less open to question.[14] But what of the occasions when accounts speak of large bodies of men in attendance at public meetings and make no specific reference to women? This was a common practice right into the Chartist period when women were almost certainly attending all public meetings in large numbers, but even speakers who were accustomed to addressing women's meetings, men such as John Fielden or Richard Oastler, would frequently treat a mixed audience as though it were composed entirely of men.

With accounts of riots, the tendency was similarly to describe their composition in terms of the number of men involved, unless women were particularly prominent and commanded attention and a mention. And so determining the composition of riot crowds presents some difficulties. Accounts of Swing riots which reached the Home Office in 1830 – 1 usually employ some blanket term such as 'mob' or 'lower orders' or the more helpful one of 'labourers', but they frequently specify that the people whose activities are being described are men. This leads to the not surprising inference that women played very little part in the riots;[15] yet it is possible that the evidence is misleading, that writers describe only the activities of men because these are the only ones which they consider to be important and that women are present who do not merit a mention. If the intention of the writer is to emphasise the seriousness of the riots he is describing he would be inclined to talk about the men who were present, for to identify women as participants was the standard means of playing down an event and suggesting that it need not be taken seriously.

The same problem arises in the study of trade disputes within occupations and industries where women are known to have been present in large numbers. Strikes within such contexts are frequently described without any reference to women's support or involvement, yet it frequently seems reasonable to assume that strikes would not have been possible if female as well as male employees were not participating. It is also true that addresses to 'fellow-workmen', which contain not a single reference to women, might none the less have been intended to embrace both sexes, just as the language of the crafts and guilds in the eighteenth century implied a totally male membership when this was not in fact the case.[16]

The identification and the counting of women are difficult exercises. Usually women are simply names, and press accounts are unlikely to indicate whether they are paupers or possessors of vast fortunes, employed or not in work, married or single. Occasionally a little more is learned about a woman if her public appearances cause her private life to come under scrutiny. It was the fate of Mrs Grassby of Elland, prominent campaigner against the New Poor Law and on behalf of Chartism, to have her marital relations discussed in the popular press because these were thought to be an area where she was vulnerable to attack. She countered the abuse by setting the record straight, at the same time telling more about herself than is usually known of the women activists.[17] Fuller exposure was usually the consequence of arrest, indictment and trial, but even there the resulting information is very thin. An investigation of Scottish protestors was hampered by the fact that women were described in terms of their relationship to a named male and that it was his occupation that was stated rather than that of the women themselves.[18] Apart from any injustice caused to the women through failure to judge and record them for what they were, this left a very incomplete record and would inevitably frustrate future attempts to analyse the women in terms of occupational status.

Even where some quantification is possible, and the same Scottish women permitted some calculation of their contribution to the totals of people tried for particular kinds of popular protest, the evidence must be treated with caution and reservations. The proportion of women participating in protest is not necessarily the same as the proportion arrested, and there is some evidence of a reluctance to arrest women; the proportion brought to trial may differ from the proportion arrested, and it is virtually impossible to know if those factors inhibiting arrest were present at this later stage of proceedings; and the equality of the sexes before the law, judged by a readiness to convict and punish the two sexes equally, is not something that can be taken for granted. Even where women are arrested, tried, convicted and sentenced to transportation for food rioting, for instance, they remain elusive, even to the point of disappearance, for George Rudé's analysis of convicts who arrived in Australia contains no women transported for food rioting, despite the sentence passed on several for this offence during the period under examination. There are several points at which they could have vanished; they could have been pardoned and released or they could have died in any of the intermediate stages that lay between their conviction and their arrival in Australia.

It is too much to hope that information will ever be complete on such issues as these, but it will at least be possible to learn a great deal more than is currently known, from further work on police and court records, from the familiar mountain of Home Office papers that doubtless has undiscovered women lurking upon its slopes, and from the columns of local newspapers which probably recorded events still awaiting publicity and wider recognition.

Inside this man's world there were obvious opportunities for women within certain social groups to be involved in some kinds of activity which were sometimes vaguely political, like the meeting of the ladies of Sheffield in May 1838, over the issue of negro emancipation.[19] This would be regarded as a philanthropic rather than a political endeavour, and the category of 'good works' was indeed one that permitted women to engage themselves in public undertakings without incurring public censure. A Bradford Female Society, for instance, was formed in 1812 to promote Christianity among Jews, at a time when local Luddites evidently felt that there were more pressing matters requiring urgent attention;[20] and in the same year the ladies of High Wycombe joined forces with the gentlemen of that town to work for the establishment of a Lancastrian School.[21] In 1819 the ladies of Manchester established a society for 'encouraging female servants', but how they were to be encouraged and to what ends were not made clear.[22] Work undertaken in connection with the local church or chapel was another outlet that was possibly more catholic in its capacity to embrace people from different social groups, women like those who ran stalls at the Church Bazaar in Leeds in February 1838, or those who 'furnished and presided over' the 64 trays which provided refreshment at the opening of the Bradford Temperance Hall in the same year.[23] These women were presumably in danger of being corrupted by contacts with Chartism, for the temperance movement disseminated much radical thinking that placed it beyond the range of activities conventionally acceptable. Much safer were the good deeds of the ladies of Leeds in February 1842, who were engaged in distributing what was called 'bounty', which consisted mainly of articles of clothing, presumably second-hand, given out to the 'deserving poor'.[24] The undeserving poor were probably too much preoccupied with politics, striking and rioting in that year to remain worthy recipients of such benefactions. It is with the activities of the latter, where they included women, that these chapters are concerned, and not with those women whose charitable endeavours met with social approval.

Any examination of women's protest during an age of Industrial Revolution must at least look for possible connections between the growth of women's protest and the course of economic change. Although women's protest clearly pre-dates industrialisation, it seems inconceivable that it did not, along with social protest in general, undergo some change in character as a result of the Industrial Revolution. Women have long been at the centre of a great range of controversies concerning the social consequences of industrialisation, its responsibility for the alleged destruction of the family, the deterioration in the health of its workers, the declining morals of the women in the work-force, and their neglect of their homes, their families and their various domestic duties and skills in consequence of their industrial employment. These debates have usually ended in compromise and an acceptance of the selective nature of the evidence that points dramatically to one extreme conclusion or another, but there is still a need to look for links between the Industrial Revolution and the growing involvement of women in a wider range of social and political protest activity. It would, for instance, be particularly useful to know more about the female activists, to be able to relate them to jobs and occupations as well as to age and status groups which are often the limit of the readily available information. Regrettably, they are frequently just 'women', who can sometimes be related to the occupational group of the men to whom they are married.

The course of women's employment patterns and the effect of the Industrial Revolution on their role within the work-force are not easy to determine. It could no longer be supposed that women first became industrial workers when the Industrial Revolution brought them into the cotton and woollen mills, for it was long ago demonstrated that they were already then a vital part of the economy in both primary producing and manufacturing sectors.[25] The extent of their pre-industrial involvement has, indeed, prompted the speculation that the coming of industrialisation, far from extending their employment opportunities, did in fact reduce them.[26] Certainly there are no easy assumptions to be made about the impact of the Industrial Revolution upon the availability of jobs for women.

Even within the textile trades, particularly within the cotton industry which is commonly supposed to have made advances possible for so many women, the position is less than certain. The dramatic growth of the cotton industry in the late eighteenth and early nineteenth centuries is believed to have created large numbers of jobs for women and children as the early factory masters turned to them to supply a cheap and convenient labour force when men were at first reluctant to move into factories. Although they were largely exluded from spinning and confined to subsidiary processes in the early stages, they outnumbered men in cotton factories at the time of the Factory Commissioners' Report of 1833 and were already taking an almost exclusive control of power-loom weaving, which would give them mastery of one of the two basic operations of the manufacture. In 1834 there were 65,000 women in cotton factories, and over 102,000 in the adult labour force in all textile mills, compared with almost 89,000 men.[27]

But it was not only factory employment that expanded women's opportunities. The spinning revolution was supported by an enormous expansion of handloom weaving, which did not reach its peak until the middle of the 1820s, and this trade, mainly a domestic one, came to employ large numbers of women. By 1800 the number of female weavers was rapidly growing in Scotland and the north and west of England, and was believed to equal the number of men, traditionally the weavers, in many places.[28] The great demand for weavers to handle the vast amounts of yarn now being produced, the loss of some male labour to the war and the need of women to find a substitute for the home spinning which they had lost all helped to push women into this employment, where they remained, after the great demand for their labour had died, part-time, casually employed, and fighting a losing battle with power-loom weaving on starvation rates which permitted neither their personal survival nor that of their declining trade.[29] The fate of the handloom weavers, called into being and allowed a transitory prosperity by the Industrial Revolution, is a warning against easy generalisations about the fate of individual groups, let alone textile workers as a whole, and the need always to balance losses against gains, over time and between groups. Before the great expansion, argued Ivy Pinchbeck, women had been involved at home in all the early cotton processes; by 1830, cleaning, carding, roving and spinning had all been taken over by the factory and spinning had become almost entirely a man's job.[30]

The advent of power-spinning, it has been demonstrated, must have caused tremendous dislocation to family economies throughout the north of England, as extremely widespread domestic spinning of cotton, wool and worsted had in the eighteenth century provided a supplementary income to the wives of men, such as labourers and lead-miners, who were themselves outside the trade. Not all women were able to move into weaving or into factory jobs, and much unemployment must have resulted. Similarly, it has been argued, the disappearance of textile outwork from the south and east of England helped to create decaying areas and was a part cause of the rural poverty associated with these areas in the early nineteenth century.[31] And even though the cotton industry created tens of thousands of new jobs and massive employment opportunities for women in both factories and homes, at least whilst the weaving boom lasted, these opportunities were concentrated heavily in particular regions, to the impoverishment of others. It has even been suggested that if textile industries are viewed as a whole, they might be seen to have had a net loss in the number of jobs available to women between the mid-eighteenth and mid-nineteenth centuries.[32]

If handloom weaving, and the employment opportunities that it extended to women, rose and fell during the eighteenth and nineteenth centuries, the same is true of outwork trades in general, though at different times and at different rates according to the industry. It may be true that the hand trades, in the end, succumbed to the factories and that the resulting technological or structural unemployment affected more people than had jobs generated for them in the nineteenth century, but in the shorter run the process was more complex.[33] As outwork was disappearing, from textiles, it has been said, it was at the same time increasing in hosiery, clothes manufacture, lace, straw, footwear and glove manufacture. In 1861 nearly one-quarter of the occupied women, 107,000, compared with 30,000 men, were working in the clothing trades in London alone, and for England and Wales, 286,000 women and girls worked as milliners and dressmakers, which was four times the number of shirtmakers and ten times the number of seamstresses. During the second half of the century the clothing trade slowly expanded, relying on outwork and an increasing proportion of women workers, and it was only the mass-produced clothing around Leeds, Manchester, Sheffield and Newcastle which kept outwork alive in the north of England by this stage. Outwork, characterised now by stitching and sewing and the assembling of separate pieces into a whole, was light work, cheap work, and work done by women, for the three were interdependent. And just as most outworkers were women, so were most women who worked in industrial occupations outworkers; they were in no sense a formal industrialised proletariat.[34]

These sweated trades, hardly a testimony to the beneficial opportunities provided for women by the Industrial Revolution, survived in many cases into the twentieth century. Others, like nail-making, reached their peak earlier and went into decline. In 1830 there were believed to be around 50,000 outworkers in this trade, which came to be increasingly dominated by women workers on low wages as it followed the familiar pattern of a losing struggle to compete against other forms of production.[35] The general nine-teenth-century trend in many metal trades was also, it has been argued, that of 'a clear shrinkage of opportunities', though in the short run the appearances were otherwise.[36] The Factory Commissioners were told around Birmingham of the trend to replace male labour by the cheaper work of women, and in the 1840s women comprised between 80 and 90 per cent of workers in the screw trade, stamping brass nails and other small metal goods.[37] The manufacture of pins, pens, buttons, pottery and matches provided other jobs, besides the crippling occupation of lock-making, described by Disraeli in *Sybil*, which created one woman worker with a back like a grasshopper because of 'the cramping posture of their usual toil'.[38]

Agiculture was another principal area for women's employment in the eighteenth century, though much of the work was unpaid, and in the nineteenth century too women played a vital role. There were great regional variations, but women worked on the land all over England, from Devonshire to Northumberland, and played an even more central role in parts of Scotland and Wales, where their capacity to perform equally with men was more readily assumed.[39] In agriculture too the picture is confused. Women are said to have found some compensation for the decline of domestic textile work, in some areas, in increased opportunities in farm work, especially in wartime, and others have noted the growth of a new class of female agricultural day labourers from around 1800 as well as the increased use of women and children in the 'gang system' which prevailed in Lincolnshire, Huntingdonshire, Cambridgeshire, Norfolk, Suffolk, Nottinghamshire, Bedfordshire and North-amptonshire.[40] Of the independent female labourers, approximately 50 per cent were dairy women, earning £8 – 10 per year, the others being outdoor labourers, farm servants or autonomous farmers.[41] Women were said to have a special aptitude for hop-picking.[42] Market gardening made much use of female labour, and at the beginning of the nineteenth century large numbers worked in the fruit and vegetable markets around London.[43] In the Scottish Highlands women shared the heaviest manual work, shearing, threshing, winnowing, raking manure, digging potatoes or hoeing turnips.[44]

But even the hard work of farming began to provide fewer opportunities for women's employment. From perhaps the middle of the century, women's agricultural labour was on the decline, from 144,000 in 1851 to 50,000 in 1881, and by the end of the century women had virtually disappeared as wage earners from agriculture.[45] Women's fluctuating opportunities for work offered by the textile trades in their various stages of transition and outwork trades which rose and fell were not stabilised by any capacity by women to take control of that oldest of all industries, agriculture. Indeed, the only real stability in trends and opportunities seems to be located in the prodigious rise in the number of women in domestic service during the nineteenth century, an occupation that was no more than a by-product of industrialisation. In 1831, there were 670,491 female domestic servants, in 1851 there were 971,000, and by 1881 1,545,000.[46] If women's work opportunities rose in the nineteenth century, this was the employment that made it possible, though domestic service seems a far cry from the liberating processes of industrialisation that are supposed to have been at work, creating a new race of independent, emancipated women.

The reservations that can be expressed about all the major areas of women's employment, except domestic service, have prompted the speculation that in the short run the Industrial Revolution could well have restricted rather than expanded women's role within the labour force. Changes in both old and new sectors of the economy did not, it is suggested, cater for the extra women generated by the demographic revolution, and the result of this, in the mid-Victorian period, was a reservoir of superfluous women, unemployed, potential cheap labour in excess of existing demands. Over the period 1851 – 81, adult women are said to have constituted almost one-third of the entire population, yet only one-fifth of these people were in recorded employment.[47] This is a sobering thought for anyone seeking to develop the case that economic independence for women was a consequence of industrialisation.

The case has none the less been made that industrialisation, in the short term and the long term, had highly beneficial consequences for women. Engels believed that capitalism undermined the basis for traditional male supremacy and Marx that industry would provide for a higher form of family relations as well as improved relations between the sexes.[48] Ivy Pinchbeck saw an improved status for those who worked outside the home, lighter work for the factory woman despite its inconveniences; for those within the home the relief from a domestic workshop, the opportunity to concentrate on home-making, and greater leisure; in the long run a much superior position for all women.[49] A long-term view has also been taken by R. M. Hartwell, who believes that the emancipation of women began with the opportunities offered by jobs in industry, and Harold Perkin, who extols the qualities promoted by factory work in the short term and identifies higher standards of living and women's emancipation as long-term consequences of industrialisation.[50] Ironically, the Industrial Revolution is also accredited with inspiring the view that a man's wage should be sufficient for a family and that a woman was therefore freed to look after the home.[51] This view will receive little sympathy from modern women, and it is one of the paradoxes of the debate that the gains of industrialisation for women are seen in terms of both the escape from the house and the ability to retreat into it, for there were women who were happy to do the one and others who were pleased to do the other.

Part of the problem of reconciling these views with the apparently limited job opportunities available to nineteenth-century women is that of distinguishing between short-term and long-term consequences. In the short-run it is difficult to see how the supposed advantages arising from industrialisation could have been widespread; in the long run, in a period that runs to the middle of the twentieth century, anything is possible, though the causal links with the Industrial Revolution become increasingly difficult to establish. Another problem is the apparent readiness to regard the factory workers as typical of women workers as a whole, when, as R. S. Neale reminds us, women in well paid work were only a minority and the majority were in low-paid occupations, frequently accepting casual work at whatever wage was offered, having low expectations and consequently low attainment.[52] And not even the much-vaunted female factory worker has gone unchallenged as a symbol of female progress. John Foster has suggested that the extent of the employment of mothers and children was an indication of the serious nature of the problem of hunger in working-class families during the early nineteenth century and labelled the working mothers as an 'alternative form of impoverishment'.[53] Edward Thompson not unreasonably asks if excessive hours of toil, bad housing, endless childbearing and high infant mortality really support the claim of an enhanced status;[54] and R. S. Neale stresses the continuing dependence and subordination, in law and in fact, of those working-class women in textile areas where women's independence has frequently been supposed to have existed.[55]

It seems unlikely then that any clear thesis can be enunciated that relates the economic progress of women with their role in social and political protest during the first half of the nineteenth century. There is no generalisation possible about the economic fortunes of nineteenth-century women, and it would be strange if their social and political behaviour were to be any more amenable to an all-embracing definition. Some tentative differentiation has already been attempted. The increasing demand for women's labour in spinning mills and handloom weaving during the war years, 1793 – 1815, has been offered as an explanation of the widespread involvement of working-class women in political and social agitation, particularly the parliamentary reform movement of 1819.[56] Conversely, it has been argued that as the outwork industries came to rely increasingly on female labour from the middle of the century, so were the direct links weakened between outwork and radical politics.[57] The one view accords women an active role of some potential importance; the other assumes that women's presence was necessarily inhibiting. What does, however, seem possible is that certain kinds of social and political response were a direct product of industrialisation, that some new forms of employment produced a disproportionately large number of female activists whereas other, perhaps larger, groups produced very few.

Factory owners, for a variety of reasons, found women's labour very attractive, and it was the women factory workers who, despite the exploitation that can be taken for granted in a situation where production took place at the lowest possible cost, enjoyed higher wages than their domestic counterparts, an absence from home that promoted social contacts, a 'liberating of the spirit' and the 'development of female moral energies' reported by the Commissioners on handloom weaving in 1840.[58] As part of the mainstream of industrial development and activity in the early nineteenth century, women would inevitably share in the experiences and grievances that these generated and in the campaigns that they precipitated. The factory population was perhaps not typical of the general population of mid-nineteenth-century Britain, but the factory towns were often the areas where working-class protest was most active and most organised. It could be argued that the new industrial areas of the North and the Midlands were the disturbed districts because of the working men who lived there, but they simultaneously produced great numbers of female radicals and protestors. Perhaps the higher wages of the factory-earning women and their close contact with organised working-class industrial and political protest encouraged them to feel a sense of their own importance and to participate themselves in the activities of male workers.

It would be interesting to speculate if these industrial areas give rise to forms of women's protest particularly concerned with economic grievance, in contrast, perhaps, with a female radicalism in London that inclined more towards civil liberty-type issues such as the campaign for a free press, the political aspects of Chartism and the concern for women's rights. Within these industrial areas themselves it will eventually be necessary to know if the women of the factories or those of the domestic industries were the more active, and whether the more violent industrial and political enterprises of the outworkers, handloom weavers or framework knitters, for instance, described by E. P. Thompson, were essentially men's campaigns, with women workers little involved. Certainly, it would be difficult to argue that women played any large part in either Luddism or the abortive revolutionary movements of the early nineteenth century. The 'slave-like' existence of those women who belonged to the trades that were successively expanded and then depressed by the Industrial Revolution, of which weaving and hosiery are outstanding examples, might well have brought apathy rather than enthusiasm in its wake. The female framework knitter observed by Felkin in 1844 to be working a 16-hour day for clear wages of 2s 6d would have little time or energy for protest;[59] no more would the female cotton handloom weavers who were working up to 14 hours a day for as little as four shillings a week on occasions.[60]

Nor were the other major areas of women's employment apparently conducive to political consciousness or female militancy. Domestic service, which employed twice as many women as all the textile trades together in 1851, presented few opportunities for organised response to its own special forms of female exploitation as isolated and scattered women tolerated the indignities of their more genteel jobs. Their wages were as low as the £8 per year paid to June Stephens, whose lot was recorded in the *English Chartist Circular* in March 1841. For this she worked a 16-hour day.[61] More fortunate women could earn up to £40 per year as ladies' maids. Occasional, short-lived attempts at trade union organisation were made, but on the whole the domestic servants had to be content with their own forms of informal protest, sulking, time-wasting, or the spoiling of food, furniture or clothing.[62] More physical, but equally unstimulating, was the agricultural work that gave employment to tens of thousands of other women in farming, market gardening or crofting within the peasant economy of the Scottish Highlands or in much of Wales. Here might be expected the so-called 'pre-industrial' and 'prepolitical' response of women concerned with the immediate necessities of life, food to eat and a place to live, and it could reasonably be expected that food rioting, anti-enclosure movements and anti-eviction riots would continue to characterise behaviour in these areas when others had turned to more sophisticated techniques of political campaigning.

And in the great sweated trades — such as those of the slop-workers, making shirts for sixpence per day, seamstresses, earning between 2s and 3s 6d per week for a 15-hour day,[63] the hat-makers, straw-plaiters, cushion lace-makers and all those other employments of the garrets, back-rooms and workshops identified by the 1842 Children's Employment Commissioners, where countless women toiled endlessly for negligible pay — mental stimulus and physical energy, the required components of political activism, would forever be wanting in this period. The brief organisation of the bonnet-makers in 1834 was exceptional.[64]

The Industrial Revolution did not initiate women's employment within the industrial work-force, but it certainly placed new demands on women, and it is ironical that a society that was ascribing new duties to women was simultaneously prescribing an ideal of a woman who belonged at home, looking after her husband and children and practising only the domestic virtues. In Harriet Martineau's view 'every girl has an innate longing . . . for the household arts, if nature had but her way', and Peter Gaskell romanticised the hallowed character of motherhood, depraved and perverted by unnatural employment outside the home.[65] Francis Place, frequently censured of late for leading the working classes along paths favoured by their social superiors, encouraged women to move in the same direction:

> I have always deprecated the employment of women in every regularly conducted trade. Women have enough to do to attend to their homes, their husbands, their children, their relatives, and such light labour as can be done at home; their place is home; there they must be or there can be no satisfaction, no comfort. All is turned upside down, when the woman is turned out of her home and turned into a mill or workshop . . . until depravity has reached its lowest depth.[66]

At the same time that the practice of women's experience was making social protest increasingly probable, the social ideal was inhibiting this kind of response and requiring other sorts of behaviour from women. All forms of industrial employment were a departure from the social ideal that was increasingly enunciated by middle-class reformers, and the champions and protectors of women from the rigours of industrial work became, ironically, as destructive of the notion of women's rights as industrial employment itself. The campaign for a Ten Hour Day was not greeted with uniform enthusiasm by female factory workers, and the defiance of mines legislation to exclude women from underground work is further indication of the ambiguity that surrounds these issues and the ambivalent views with which social benefactors were regarded.[67] Whilst their patrons sought to confine them to their homes and domestic duties the women themselves, in embarking upon their campaigns of protest, frequently found it necessary to argue that their political involvement was not distracting them from their duties or detracting from their performance as wives or mothers. They continued to show deference to the principle whilst they practised behaviour that ran contrary to its precepts.

And if they were frustrated in whatever legitimate career aspirations they were holding and in their capacity to act politically by the ideal of their would-be protectors, they were equally frustrated by the male opposition which they encountered on both fronts. Male hostility to the cheap, often docile, labour which they offered, which resulted in their exclusion from jobs and trade unions and occasional violence from male workers, also carried over into politics. Although there was some male encouragement received in 1819 and their support was actually canvassed during the Chartist period, the unease felt at the unaccustomed female presence in the political arena persisted throughout the period and compelled women to adopt defensive and self-deprecating attitudes whenever they ventured to make themselves heard. They did nevertheless begin to make themselves heard. Within industry, within society and within politics, working women suffered all the disadvantages and grievances of working men, and more besides, because of their sex. They were therefore driven, despite any inhibitions about their right to be in employment and their right to do anything to improve their lives, into actions of various kinds. In a period when there were few opportunities for nursing, teaching and clerical work, the careers suggested by Harriet Martineau in 1859, it was working-class women of the industrial work-force who were the organisers of and participators in the protest movements of the first half of the century.[68]

This is a descriptive account of the activities of women, mainly working-class, in a variety of social and political activities that can be broadly categorised as 'protest'. It is an indication of the type of activities in which women participated. It establishes some broad outlines and a few landmarks, and offers an interpretation of the course of events as they are at present known. It also raises questions which remain to be answered, especially the basic ones of what happened and why. It does not aspire to being a comprehensive account of such activities, for it would be very naïve to suppose that anyone was in a position to provide such an account. The recent historiography of food rioting has afforded a salutary example to all in this respect. As long as the number of identified late-eighteenth- or early-nineteenth-century food riots continues to grow at an alarming rate, no one of discretion is going to be willing to suppose that knowledge of the events is complete, let alone the capacity to interpret them.[69] The lesson of the food riots seems to be that they are not found in places where they are not sought, which is hardly surprising, and that it will be time enough to produce a final count when every place has been searched. There are still sufficient places left and sufficient paper to be read to postpone any such reckoning for some time yet.

Similarly with women's social and political activities: they are found only in those areas where they are sought, and when they are found the pattern of the discoveries suggests that the location and importance of events have been discovered, when only certain locations and certain events have even been investigated. There are obvious starting points for investigations, but they are no more than starting points. It seems sensible, for instance, to look at Lancashire and West Yorkshire as known areas of intense industrial and political activity, but the evidence that they will supply will give an impression rather than an understanding of what the whole picture may eventually be. The scene is constantly changing as we come to know more and more about more and more. These chapters are a sample of the available material, and as such they offer only tentative conclusions about a subject of enormous proportions.

2 WOMEN IN FOOD RIOTS

Such a reputation as women had for taking an active part in social protest prior to 1800 was derived very largely from food rioting and involvement in a variety of price-fixing operations. Recent historians have been suitably cautious in ascribing to women a role that identifies them entirely with the home and family and have given timely warnings that women were involved in more than 'bread and butter' issues.[1] Nevertheless, they find it difficult to resist the conclusion that it was woman as the protector of the domestic economy, the defender of her family's well-being, who was in the vanguard of female protest. In this role women had long resorted to verbal and even physical violence in their endeavours to force prices down and ensure an equitable distribution of food in times of scarcity, and they would continue active in a wide range of early-nineteenth-century food riots throughout England, Scotland and Wales. And when the threat to the home went beyond the question of food supply, when enclosures or land clearance threatened to dispossess the family of its house or land or Poor Law officials attempted to split up families in workhouses, other issues arose which extended the range of women's action.

But it was in food rioting, described as a form of 'pre-industrial' and 'pre-political' behaviour, where they stood out, and this whole phenomenon is now much better understood as a result of recent investigations.[2] The many forms that it took, the attacks on particular kinds of property and particular kinds of persons, the stopping of carts, boats and barges, have now been described in some detail; the participants have to some extent been identified, specific groups of industrial workers as well as women, youths and 'the poor' in general, and their targets labelled. Food rioters have also been provided with an ideology in terms of the 'moral economy' that they sought to preserve against the freely operating market forces that were in ascendancy by the end of the eighteenth century. A rationale has thus been given for food rioting by E. P. Thompson in much the same way that E. J. Hobsbawm made sense for the first time of machine breaking as 'collective bargaining by riot'.

Scholars have also suggested that food riots occurred particularly when food prices rose sharply rather than when they were at their highest and that short-term price movements and shortages were more important than long-term trends capable of inducing famine or starvation. Regional studies have helped to substantiate these views. Riots occurred in heavy concentrations through periods of shortage, 1795 – 6, 1800 – 1, 1810 – 3 and 1816 – 18, becoming less numerous through the successive crises until they were superseded by other forms of popular protest. They lingered on in the 'fringe' areas such as the Scottish Highlands and Cornwall, which had its last major outbreak in 1847, but the declining importance of food rioting as a form of popular action within an increasingly industrial society had already been foreshadowed by shifts within the distribution of the riots themselves. Whereas, it has been suggested, eighteenth-century riots tended to occur on the coast, at canal and river ports, and market towns near large population concentrations, succeeding outbreaks were more associated with the industrial and manufacturing centres of the north and Midlands, whose non-food producing workers were handicapped initially by transport defects.[3] Having taken over the food riot, the industrial workers would soon reject it in favour of other means of conduct, but in the meantime the women of the country towns and villages would be complemented by those of the industrial areas in their participation in this form of social protest.

The course of industrial change is clearly a factor of the greatest importance in the history of food rioting, as it is indeed for the whole history of women's involvement in social and political protest of all kinds, and recent studies of food riots contain an important lesson for the study of women's involvement. It now seems probable that the shift of food rioting into the industrial centres occurred earlier than was once supposed, that earlier geographical interpretations of food rioting are now more questionable, and that food riots were more common in the eighteenth century than used to be supposed. It may be that women's well established role in food rioting will undergo a change of interpretation when the riots themselves have all been identified. Meanwhile, it is necessary to consider it in the light of recent novel suggestions that have been made about the nature of food rioting; that it had become associated with questions of wages and unemployment as early as 1795; that food rioters, at least in the northeast of England, were showing a fairly high level of political consciousness by 1800 and associating their economic grievances with political radicalism; and that food rioting was already, by the end of the eighteenth century, ceasing to have a purely independent existence and would increasingly be mixed up with other forms of social protest, such as Luddism, in the future.[4] If these hypotheses, already in part substantiated, should secure general acceptance, it may well be difficult to sustain both the growing politicisation of food rioting and the accepted view of women within it. Alternatively, it may be possible to show that women's involvement in food rioting in fact moved them towards political involvement sooner than has been generally supposed. In a fluid situation the only certainty seems to be that all judgements are destined to become quickly out of date.

Another problem is that at the same time as food rioting was possibly becoming caught up in other 'forward-looking' forms of protest related to the manufacturing areas, it continued to display signs that it was a form of 'collective reactionary violence', concerned to preserve the old ways and the old days when 'forestalling, engrossing, and regrating' were crimes against society and the pursuit of profit was not the supreme aim of social management.[5] Repeated examples of food riots designed to prevent the movement of food from one part of the country to another were acts of resistance to the establishment of a single market economy. Perhaps the women were particularly reluctant to accept economic changes and the changing philosophy that accompanied them, for as late as 1830 the Mevagissey 'female dealers in fish', who were so conspicuous in grain riots at their port, were criticised for their erroneous thoughts, said to be 'founded on ignorance that would insulate each district, and bring us back to the state of things under the Saxon Heptarchy'.[6]

For the time being, at any rate, women remain the commonly accepted historians' choice for the leaders of food riots of the late eighteenth and early nineteenth centuries. E. P. Thompson, citing many examples of women's leadership in the eighteenth century, expresses the view that the initiators of riots were very often women and believes it probable that women were most frequently responsible for precipitating spontaneous actions.[7] Others have noted the prominence of women in the early nineteenth century and quoted with approval the view of the *Leicester Journal*, in 1800, that 'all public disturbances generally commence with the clamour of women and the folly of boys'.[8] In Wales women were said to be among the most vocal and extreme of food rioters, and their regular appearance believed to be one of the most interesting features of riots in that country.[9] Similarly in Scotland, women's participation and leadership have attracted special noting.[10] Certainly, there were plenty of incidents to support this kind of view. In 1800, at Lane End, a woman ringing a bell rallied a crowd of women who proceeded to stop and unload food carts that were bound for Newcastle-under-Lyme,[11] and on Boxing Day of that year three women led a popular attack on a ship at Kircudbright that was due to take potatoes to the people of Liverpool.[12] During the troubles of 1812 women continued to be very prominent. They gave leadership to market disturbances in Manchester and Macclesfield,[13] and the 'poor misguided creatures' who took part in the Sheffield food riots of August were said to have been principally led on by women.[14] During the Nottingham food riots of September 'one of the assailing divisions bore a woman in a chair, who gave the word of command, and was dignified with the title of Lady Ludd', and a similar thing had happened in Leeds the previous month.[15] There a party of women and boys had also been led by a woman with the name of Lady Ludd and had paraded the streets, attacking meal shops and millers' premises. Less flamboyant was Betty, the wife of John Wood of Horbury, near Wakefield, who in June, 'did riotously upset a cart containing potatoes and onions . . . which said property was feloniously and forcibly taken away'. Betty raised the crowd against the owner, crying, 'Damn him, let us murder him and take his stuff from him' and in other ways aided and abetted in the riot. She was charged along with Mary Ellis and Mary Wright, and Benjamin Byron had to come to court to tell how 'a number of women and children made an assault upon him and threw his potatoes into the street'.[16]

The large food riots in Ely, Bury St Edmunds, Brandon and Downham, in East Anglia, 1816, were also characterised by determined female activity and obvious leadership. Ann Folkes and Helen Dyer were arrested for their part in the great Brandon riot, where an estimated 1,500 paraded with flags and pikes; the latter explained that, although unable to read, she had none the less carried a paper containing the crowd's demands which she wanted to deliver to the magistrate. They posed the now familiar alternatives, 'Bread or Blood in Brandon this day'. In Downham, Hannah Jarvis, along with three men, led the crowd which robbed George Thomas of several gallons of beer, and she alone led an attack on a butcher's shop, where she distributed beef among the crowd.[17]

Such conduct, frequently recorded in times of food rioting, has prompted the judgement that women were more numerous and more active than men in this form of social protest, despite the absence of statistical evidence to support this case.[18] There is certainly a good deal of subjective observation that supports this view, but the question must remain open. It seems likely that women were less liable to be arrested and prosecuted than men, for reasons to be discussed, but it remains highly unlikely that women's participation in riots can be adequately quantified. And so long as that is true, it remains a possibility that the prominence of women was more apparent than real.

One thing that does seem certain is that whatever weight women threw into food riots, either as leaders or as supporters, they were widely recognised as *agents provocateurs* who incited men to greater action. At Haverfordwest in 1795, colliers, on their way to unload a ship carrying butter, were urged on by women, and during corn riots at Beaufort in 1800, when iron miners and colliers had taken possession of a load of barley meal, it was a woman who urged them to rip open the sacks and drive the horses into the furnaces, an exhortation which they were apparently able to resist.[19] In October, another woman was charged with encouraging people to break bakers' windows during the food riots in Margate.[20] Some went further than this. When a riot occurred in Llandidloes in May 1839, after the authorities attempted to arrest ten persons accused of stealing beef and other food items from local farmers, women were said to have been during the whole commotion 'most active in inciting the men by their cries, and carrying them stones'.[21] Occasionally too there were cases of incitement to inactivity by women against the soldiers who sometimes had the task of suppressing food riots. In August 1795, Colonel Entwistle of the Rochdale Volunteers complained to the Home Office that

> the Devil in the shape of women is using all his influence to induce the privates to brake [sic] their attachment to their officers, and I am sorry to add has already debouched three from their duty, by delivering up their arms and accoutrements.[22]

This exploitation of their sex appears to have achieved more dramatic results for the Lancashire women than those of

Haverfordwest in the same year who attempted to beguile the soldiery there by telling them 'that they knew they were in their hearts for them and would do them no hurt'.[23] More frequently no quarter was sought or given by women.

The relative importance of male and female contributions to food rioting is not easy to determine. The numerous occasions on which women were prominent tend to suggest an impression that food rioting was essentially a woman's activity, but that is almost certainly not so, and it is the unusually large number of occasions of female activism in this area, which contrasts with female quiescence and passivity in so many others, that gives this misleading impression. If rioting women are the point of focus, then food rioting appears a woman's activity, yet for all the reported cases of female prominence there was at least an equal number of reported incidents where women received no mention. Food riots often progressed with women at their head, but they often progressed when women were not involved, or were not prominent. It is significant, though not of course by any means conclusive, that in its first twenty reports of food riots in 1800, *The Times* should have specifically mentioned women participants on only one occasion, and that was the outburst in Pontefract and district in early May.[24]

By contrast, *The Times* did identify other participating groups in these riots, the colliers and nailers who rioted at Dudley in late April on account of high prices in the markets, the colliers who rioted at Chester-le-Street in early May because of the high price of provisions, and the colliers again, of Cowpen Colliery, who passed through Blythe later in the month and 'committed many riotous acts' with the same grievance.[25] These references suggest that colliers might well be worth considering as a particularly riotously inclined group, and they certainly discredit any idea that women were needed for a food riot to take place. Furthermore, the usual interest shown in reporting the illegal activities of women suggests that they would not have been ignored had they been present in large numbers on the occasions when no reports occurred of their participation. And if, in fact, the miners are pursued further, it will be seen that on 12 September *The Times* reported riots in Chesterfield in which the miners 'fixed a maximum on every marketable article' and that on the following day it reported troubles in Coventry, when colliers, armed with bludgeons, had plundered bakers' shops.[26] In April 1812 was reported the dramatically worded news item that 'The miners have risen' near

Truro and compelled farmers to sell at fixed prices.[27] The miners, in other words, seem to have been capable of performing most of the functions usually attributable to women in food riots. And in the one statistical analysis that seems to have been made of prosecuted food rioters, it appears that only 29 per cent were women of those so prosecuted in Scotland in the late eighteenth and early nineteenth centuries.[28] Prosecution and participation figures do not necessarily correspond, but the figures do at least suggest caution. In general, it could be said that present speculations on this matter remain inconclusive and could be substantiated only by more detailed and comprehensive accounts of riots than have so far been assembled, but they are suggestive and they should inhibit any extreme judgement on food rioting as an exclusively women's protest.

For all that, food rioting was an activity in which women were prominent, and this needs to be explained, for crowds of women or crowds consisting 'chiefly of women and boys' were persistently alleged to be responsible for 'the troubles', 'the instruments', in the words of *The Times*, of more sinister forces at work behind the scenes.[29] Whatever the strength of the Reds beneath early-nine-teenth-century beds, it is evident that it was the women who had both the knowledge and the sense of obligation to detect a wrong and to attempt to rectify it. They had, as E. P. Thompson explains, the marketing experience to detect short weight and inferior quality, and they had also the custodianship of their family within their duties.[30] Couched in slightly more tendentious language is the suggestion that 'the prominence of working class women in these class struggles of the market place derives from their familial roles as executors of the wage'.[31] Hence Olwen Hufton's claim that food-rioting French women of the late eighteenth century were often mothers who had children to feed, proud people who survived in good times but struggled in times of depression to provide the necessities of life.[32] The task might require hard work and ingenuity at the best of times, but in the worst it was frustrating to the point of provoking riot and disturbances. Then a controlled and limited violence would erupt that stopped short of unlicensed robbery or murder, but made possible the exposure of a villain, the destruction of an acknowledged abuse, or, more especially, the availability in the short term of cheaper food to the immediate community. It was said, during the Nottingham riots of 1800, that with 'famine-impelled eagerness' many a mother bore away corn in her apron to feed her offspring, and this kind of comment leaves little room for further speculation.[33] Women's general involvement in food rioting presents no great puzzles. What will be of particular interest is knowlege of why certain groups of women were specially active, groups, for instance, like the wives and other female relatives of Scottish seamen who, in the absence of their male relatives, were very prominent in the food riots in Scottish coastal towns in the late eighteenth century.[34]

When they did riot, women invariably had very precise targets which recur frequently in the history of this period. Shops were often chosen for the focal point of demonstrating, particularly those of bakers and mealmen. During the troubles of late Summer and early Autumn 1800, the bakers and flour sellers of Nottingham had their premises attacked as women endeavoured to make food available, and the bakers of Margate were similarly treated.[35] In Worcester both bakers and mealmen had their premises attacked either because they had insufficient bread and flour to supply their customers or for complying with a recent Act of Parliament under which they were forbidden to sell bread less than 24 hours old.[36] In August of 1812, the millers and the flour and meal sellers all had their premises attacked in Leeds and Sheffield.[37] Equally vulnerable were market-stall owners and holders, for markets were a natural gathering place for women and places where comparisons could easily be made as well as crowds easily mobilised. At Harwich in September 1800, it was the market people who were the victims of women's action as they brought in their commodities of all kinds and had fixed prices placed upon them,[38] and the Shudehill Potato Market riots in Manchester of April 1812 formed one of the best-known examples of this kind of action as the rioting women fixed a 'sort of maximum' on the goods for sale.[39]

Sometimes people themselves were the focal point of riots. In 1800 the Mayor of Blandford is reported as having written to the Home Office to complain that his house had been surrounded by local women who were demanding food at reasonable prices.[40] As mayor he was evidently expected to do something about the problem. Usually the crowd would tackle more directly the person or persons thought to be responsible for their dilemma. In September crowds of boys and women threatened the destruction of all millers in the neighbourhood, and in Dereham, Norfolk, a few days later, one miller was singled out for ill treatment, being dragged from the inn where he had hidden himself and pelted with his own materials.[41] The reputation of early-nineteenth-century millers seems to have been no better than that of their eighteenth-century predecessors, and when they escaped personal assault they sometimes had to suffer attacks upon their houses. A 'tumultuous assemblage', consisting chiefly of women, which assembled in Lym market-place in early September 1800, proceeded to a miller's house and broke all his windows prior to entering the building and damaging the inside, a performance that was renewed the following day.[42] And in April 1812 the houses of Ayr meal dealers were attacked by crowds of women and boys who broke their windows and then their furniture.[43] During the Downham food riots of 1816 Hannah Jarvis and Amelia Lightharness led a crowd to a pork butcher's where Amelia spurred them on by shouting, 'Here my boys, this is the place for good pork!'; likewise at Ely, Sarah Hobbes selected the venue for a crowd attack on a flour and grocery shop by crying, 'Come along, come along . . . we will go to Cooper's, he is a bigger rogue than Rickwood [the miller].'[44]

Warehouses, storehouses and the mills themselves were fairly popular targets. During the Nottingham riots of August 1800 women broke into granaries at the canal wharfs,[45] and in Swansea the following April crowds of women and children broke down warehouse doors, demanding corn at a fair price.[46] In the Carlisle riots of April 1812 a body of 300 men and women carried off food from warehouses, and forty people, mainly girls, were taken into custody for the offence.[47] During the same month a mill at Barton-upon-Irwell, about six miles from Manchester, was visited by a crowd said to consist of many hundreds of rioters. Subsequently, Mary Lunn, Sarah Parkinson, Ann Hamer, Elizabeth Benyon, Mary Barlow and Mary Clare were charged with feloniously removing '8 or 10 lbs of flour'. They were all accused of having filled their aprons with flour and tests had evidently revealed that this was the average amount of flour that a woman's apron held.[48]

The other common category of target consisted of the boats, barges and carts on which food was moved from one district to another or was in transit between millers and the customers. In April 1800 a crowd of women at Lane End stopped carts that were taking food to Newcastle-under-Lyme,[49] and in October 1800 a wagon belonging to a Mr Beck of Bathwick Mill was stopped at Warmley by a crowd of 200 women. They seized and carried off fourteen sacks of flour, sending their wagoner home with a solitary horse and leaving the other three in the hands of his attackers.[50]

Carts of grain bound for Birmingham were stripped by women at Burford in 1795, as were barges that were halted by the women of Tewkesbury.[51] Canal transport seems to have featured fairly prominently as targets of riotous women. The Aire and Calder were scenes of assaults upon barges carrying grain to Leeds and Bradford, and in August 1812 women assembled at Knottingley Lock, near Pontefract, in order to intercept a vessel supposedly laden with corn. Disappointed in their quest, they assembled in Knottingley the next morning in a crowd three hundred strong and forced the meal sellers to let them have meal at their own price of 3*s* per stone.[52]

Ports featured commonly in this kind of riot. In December 1800 women of Kircudbright led an attack upon a vessel that was loaded with potatoes that were due to be taken to Liverpool,[53] and in 1830 the notorious Mevagissey fish-wives attacked farmers and wagon-drivers in an attempt to prevent the shipment of grain to an eastern port.[54] The Carlisle troubles of April 1812 had started when a crowd had left the town to visit Sandsfield, the port of the town, to unship cargoes of corn. Foiled by the army, they returned to the town, but both parties now became embroiled in physical conflict as women and boys began to throw stones at the magistrates and soldiers, who responded by drawing their swords and firing their guns, as a result of which one woman was killed and several more wounded.[55]

All these incidents give some idea of the techniques usually employed by women in food riots. The mildest, though not necessarily the least unnerving, was the hissing, often ritualised, or other forms of verbal abuse, that might constitute the preliminaries of a more physical assault. Such was the treatment given by the women of Nottingham to the Yeomen Cavalry and Infantry who had the task of maintaining order in September 1800.[56] When protest had to be stepped up it was usually done by the throwing of stones, an easily accessible weapon and one easily despatched by women at very vulnerable targets, the windows of their enemies. Stones were thrown and windows were broken in Worcester, Romsey, Lym, Margate and doubtless many other places by food-rioting women in 1800, and sometimes the stones were supplemented by volleys of mud.[57] On occasions stones were thrown at soldiers, as at Carlisle in April 1812, but this was a less effective use of them, for soldiers broke less easily than windows and retaliated with greater force.[58] At Skipton in April 1812 a potato seller was pelted by women with his own potatoes, a not unusual event, for it seemed particularly appropriate that the offender should be assailed by the offensive commodity, as the miller of Dereham discovered in 1800.[59]

The degree of violence and the degree of strength displayed by women in food riots seem to have been determined by the needs of the situation rather than any inherent physical weakness of the female sex. If verbal taunts or stone-throwing were sufficient, then these were all that occurred. If, however, market stalls needed to be overturned, then women were quite ready and able to overturn them. If wagons had to be stopped and sacks of flour carried away, as at Warmley in October 1800, then fourteen sacks of flour and three horses could evidently be removed as and when the need arose.[60] And if it was a case of direct physical confrontation between soldiers and an assembly of women, then this too was not beyond their courage. Clashes between the army and the crofters' wives of the Scottish Highlands will be considered later, but even in the English lowlands women were not lacking to offer a direct challenge to armed soldiers. When, during the course of the Nottingham food riots of August/September 1800, some twenty to thirty young male prisoners were brought into the town from Arnold in an open wagon, 'the women would have gladly effected a rescue but were overpowered by the soldiery.'[61] If food rioting was woman's work, so too was fighting; and it would be difficult to argue that a crowd of angry women behaved typically in a more restrained, less violent manner than a crowd of angry men. There is plenty of evidence to suggest that they acted on occasion with a more passionate commitment to their purpose than comparable crowds of men.

Sometimes there appeared a peculiarly feminine flair for dramatic portrayal of protest through symbolism or panache of another kind. The 'tumultuous set of women' who rioted at Dereham in September 1800 against the high price of flour and meal also charged one miller with selling adulterated meal and to make the point more effectively 'exhibited bread and dumplings about the town'.[62] More imaginative was the behaviour of the Nottingham women in September 1812 who stuck a halfpenny loaf on top of a fishing rod, 'after having streaked it with red ochre and tied around it a shred of black crepe', emblematic, it was said, of 'bleeding famine decked in sackcloth'. With the assistance of three hand-bell ringers these women collected a large crowd, including members of the West Kent Militia, who were annoyed at having received short-weight loaves or 'tommies'. These men had earlier entered the town wearing oaken boughs or twigs in their caps to commemorate, it was said, the occasion when William the Conqueror had been stopped by the women and men of Kent who had gone to meet him carrying branches of oak. It was appropriate that the Kentish militia should again team up with protesting women against a social evil, this time under the leadership of a woman borne aloft in a chair 'who gave the word of command and was dignified with the title of Lady Ludd'.[63] Her bravado made her the spiritual descendant of the woman who had 'regaled her associates with a guinea's worth of liquor at the Crab Tree public house' after leading a brigade of women against a Sussex miller in 1801 and cutting his dressing cloth 'into a thousand pieces'.[64]

The survival of ancient ritual, even in urban settings such as London, has evoked comment in the context of women's food riots, particularly in connection with the practice of draping black crêpe over loaves and carrying them around on poles.[65] Another old practice frequently followed by food-rioting women, and clearly intended in part as a gesture of self-confidence and defiance, was to use the local bell-man to circulate news of their success and publicise their achievements. The Knottingley women who had forcibly extracted meal at three shillings per stone from the sellers then sent the bell-man around to cry the new prices.[66] Similarly, the women of one district in Bradford, who had managed to lower milk prices by a successful embargo, sent the bell-man around with the good news.[67] Bell-ringing does, of course, feature prominently in the raising of crowds. The women of Lane End, in 1800, whose action cut off the Newcastle food carts, were headed by a woman ringing a bell, and they all wore blue ribbons.[68]

At other times the ritual, the passion and the emotion were superseded by a calm, cool sense of purpose which allowed women to carry through an exercise in price-fixing with extraordinary precision and detachment. Such an occasion arose at Harwich in September 1800. As the market people came into the market with their wares, the assembled women demanded to know the prices, and on being told that butter was 1s 7d per pint, eggs 1s per dozen, potatoes 4s per bushel and onions 8d per quarter of a peck, they entered into a combination and agreed upon a different set of prices: butter was to be 1s, eggs 6d per dozen, potatoes 2s per bushel and onions 4d a quarter of a peck. The market people, having been informed of these prices, were not content, upon which 'the mob took and distributed the goods at the above rates, in the presence of the Mayor and a great number of parishioners'. And, not content with this salutary gesture, they declared their intention to do the same with bread and meat at the next market unless their price was reduced.[69]

It would probably be premature to attempt too detailed a discussion of what kind of women took part in food riots. If the 'faces in the crowd' have been a long time appearing with any clarity, the same is equally true of the female faces in the crowd. In fact, the faces of the women in the crowd are even more indistinct because their owners were invariably categorised when caught according to their single or married status rather than any occupation which they followed in their own right. Whether food-rioting women tended to be housewives, people at home, or working women, perhaps doubling as housewives, it is impossible to say. In general their names are unknown, and their status, married or single, and their occupational grouping remain matters for speculation unless some observer offers a guess at the latter or the processes of law elicit the former. Nor are age patterns clearly indicated except that not many older women appear active in food riots; descriptions of rioters suggest that they can be anything from 'young girls' to women in their middle or late forties. Some of the well known views about male rioters, that they were not the very poorest, the down and out of a community, but people of some modest social status, or that they did not contain factory workers to any great extent before the 1830s, all remain to be tested where women food rioters are concerned.[70] They seem destined, even more than the men, to remain fairly obscure. Almost by definition a food rioter is likely to be someone who is poor, or at least poor enough to be in difficulties in times of shortage, and so must be expected to be found amongst the working and labouring classes of the towns and country. And in particular riots the women involved seem to have been those from the appropriate occupational groups of the area or the circumstances. In Nottingham stockingers' wives would naturally make up the riotous crowds of women; during a Glasgow miners' strike it would naturally be the miners' wives who stole potatoes from the fields.[71] In the Scottish coastal towns, where food riots most frequently occurred, the female relatives of seamen were, not surprisingly, to the fore,[72] and in the fishing village of Mevagissey it was the fish-wives who attempted to stop the movement of grain.[73] In the Truro food riots of 1812, which coincided with a stoppage in the mines, it was, as might be expected, the girls who worked 'about the mines' who were on hand to supply the female element in the food-rioting crowd.[74]

This somewhat simplistic view does not carry the analysis very far, and it is complicated a little by the cautionary tale of the commanding guards' officer communicated to the Home Secretary in 1820. When quartered at Winchester and requested by the civil authorities to call out his regiment to quell a riot in the market, he had, he claimed, declined to do this but had chosen instead to send out orders for the soldiers' wives to return home, whereupon the commotion had subsided.[75] All this really does is warn of the little that is actually known of the precise nature of the female rioters and the ingredients of riots on specific occasions.

One likely clue to a further elucidation of the role of women in food riots is to be found in the information relating to the patterns of arrests on these occasions. An analysis of food-rioting statistics in Scotland, 1780 – 1815, suggests that 28 per cent of those charged were women and that women were less likely to be charged than men.[76] If, in addition to this, it is conceded that women were a lot less likely to be arrested than were men, the inference to be drawn appears to be that women might well have made up half of food-rioting crowds and played a part in food riots equal to that of men. Difficulties in clarifying this are compounded by the need to know more about the attitude of the authorities towards food rioting as a crime as well as the possible partiality shown towards women in the administration of the law. There is plenty of evidence that food rioting was sometimes allowed to go unchecked by the authorities for several hours, as if it constituted a rough justice that could on occasions be tolerated. There is also plenty of evidence to suggest that rioting crowds, applying their own 'moral economy' to the situation, not only believed that their conduct had moral sanction, but that it had legal backing too. Crowds which had made the first assault upon property or persons might then appeal to magistrates to intercede on their behalf to negotiate or confirm a settlement already reached by use of force. The 'right' of women to raise a food riot in particular circumstances is something that cannot be entirely discounted.

This may be supported in part by the obvious reluctance of the authorities to arrest large numbers of women. It has already been suggested that they were not necessarily present in large numbers at all food riots, but, when they clearly were there in strength, they sometimes enjoyed a measure of immunity.

The magistrates of Nottingham appear to have been fairly tolerant, for on 20 July 1795

a large mob, consisting principally of women, went from one baker's shop to another, set their own price on the stock therein, and putting down the money, took it away. They were permitted to pursue this course for several hours, but the bakers becoming very clamourous for protection, the authorities at length interfered, and the riot was subdued by the assistance of the military from the Barracks, and the Gentlemen Troop of Yeomanry, who jointly scoured the streets till midnight.[77]

In early September 1800 there were further troubles and some forty or more arrests were reported on 5 September, but 'the women are the principal aggressors and they are permitted to remain at liberty'.[78] In May five men were sent to prison for rioting in the market of the same town, but no woman;[79] in August seven ring-leaders were arrested at Portsea for rioting against bread prices, and these included only one woman;[80] in the September riots at Birmingham all the reported dead and wounded were men;[81] following attacks on London shopkeepers in the same month fifteen persons were charged, and all were male;[82] and after the Sheffield food riots of 1812, when butter was stolen, six men and one woman were arrested, the woman for her part in attacking an arms store.[83] Against these must be placed other fragmentary pieces of information, the forty people, chiefly girls, arrested at Carlisle in April 1812, and the four women and one man arrested following the Manchester potato riots of the same month.[84] These items permit no more than an impression, but it is an impression that women probably experienced a little latitude when the question of making arrests was raised.

When it was a question of punishments the evidence is again far from conclusive. A recent investigation of bread riots in the north-east of England has suggested that the authorities made no distinction between the sexes in the sentences that were handed out, that punishment was strictly according to degree of involvement, and that the object was to make an example of the worst offenders irrespective of their sex. Thus the women involved in food rioting at Ashton-under-Lyme in 1800 had punishments to fit the severity of the offence; some were acquitted, Nancy Dawson was imprisoned for one month, Ellen Thompson for six months, and Mary Gartside transported for seven years 'for riotously taking possession and disposing of . . . a quantity of flour and bread and forcibly lowering its price'.[85] Four years earlier, at Hawarden, two other women received seven years' transportation for taking bags of flour from wagons.[86] At the Leicester Quarter Sessions in October 1800 one woman was given fourteen days' solitary confinement for rioting in the butter market, an apparently trivial offence, whilst another received seven years' transportation for stealing during the riot.[87] At the same time a Derby man was transported for seven years just for rioting.[88] The three women accused of food rioting at Horbury, including Betty Wood who had recommended that they should murder the handler of potatoes, were all acquitted at the York Assizes in August 1812 by a judge who dismissed the cases on the grounds that it had not been proved that the accused themselves ran away with potatoes and that they could not be held responsible for those in the crowd who had resorted to stealing.[89] Betty Wood's blatant incitement evidently amused rather than annoyed him. Across the Pennines the experiences of the female prisoners were extremely mixed. Women who were convicted of stealing flour in Bolton were given six months' hard labour and fined one shilling, whereas Mary Hurt received twelve months' imprisonment at Chester for being involved in a mob at Stalybridge which stole and destroyed upwards of 1,000 bushels of flour and meal. For the same offence her male companion was sentenced to seven years' transportation.[90] Phoebe Smith, a Manchester food rioter, was one of the luckiest of all. She was charged with having riotously assembled at the house of John Holland, of Deansgate, and being involved in the breaking of doors and windows and the stealing of bread, cheese and potatoes. The Crown appeared to have a good case against her, for she was seen by James Andrews, a constable, to have been 'active amongst the rioters' and 'busy conveying away potatoes from the shop'. Other witnesses also saw her removing potatoes, yet she was acquitted.[91]

But of all the 'ignorant and unthinking people' who participated in the Manchester food riots, Hannah Smith achieved the greatest form of notoriety. She was hanged for the crime of highway robbery, an unusually severe reprisal for behaviour that was not normally so categorised. Her offences were in fact many and prolonged, for she was first seen by witnesses at 9 o'clock on the morning of 20 April, stopping potato carts, and encouraging a crowd of more than 100 persons to take the vegetables without payment. She was seen unscrewing the side of a cart, upsetting potatoes in the street, and then filling her apron and running away. Later in the day, at 2 o'clock, she was again seen 'heading up the Mob', foremost amongst a crowd of 200 who obliged a Mr Lomas to take a loss on the retail price of his stock. Not content with this, she was subsequently seen threatening to stop butter carts and horses bringing milk into the town; owners were offered prices of 1s per pound for butter and 2d per quart for milk and told that if this was unacceptable she would have both items for nothing and was capable of raising a hundred persons to assist her. When threatened with a constable she allegedly replied:'I would have him to mind or he will be hanged up. I know he will.' Two days later Hannah Smith resumed her activities and implemented some of her earlier threats. After a butter cart had been stopped, 'the Prisoner was very active and got upon the Cart and delivered out the Butter at one shilling a Pound.' She was indicted for highway robbery, having allegedly stolen 20 lb of butter to the value of 36s and carried it away, albeit for resale to the crowd.

Her offences were numerous, for she enjoyed a full day of unrepented rioting on the 20th and returned refreshed on the 22nd, an unmistakable leader of capital crime.[92] At the closing of Lancaster Assizes in June, Baron Thompson pronounced his fearful sentence with carefully chosen words that indicated the extent of the offence:

> You, Hannah Smith, have been guilty of a robbery on the highway of a large quantity of butter, seizing the prosecutor's cart, and assisting in carrying away nearly the whole of the contents, without the owner having been paid for it; you have also been convicted of stealing a quantity of potatoes. This circumstance seems to prove that you were one of the most determined enemies to good order, and it is fit to be understood, that sex is not entitled to any mitigation of punishment, when the crime is of such a nature as to deserve it. . . [Let others] take warning from your example and observe that they cannot with impunity conspire to disturb the public tranquility.[93]

Baron Thompson had no interest in the moral economy of the

crowd, only the preservation of law and order, and those who threatened it, even though women, should expect no mercy. Hannah Smith had indeed proved herself 'one of the most determined' and by her successive efforts brought upon herself this uniquely severe penalty. Rather more fortunate were the East Anglian rioters who had contributed dramatically to the events of 1816; Amelia Lightharness and Hannah Jarvis were transported to New South Wales, perhaps to be categorised as thieves, while others received sentences of six to twelve months in gaol with hard labour.[94] Such penalties indicate the futility of a general belief in any female advantage before the law. Severe retribution was often the outcome of events in which women might have had some initial advantage over soldiers or magistrates because of their sex.

The role of early-nineteenth-century women in food rioting is clearly one of great importance, whatever the difficulties in the way of calculating just how important, and it was of long-term significance for the history of women's involvement in popular protest and politics that their principal protest activity or outlet was of declining importance as the century advanced. It has been suggested that from the very beginning of the century the food riot was on the decline as an independent phenomenon and that it would increasingly become mixed up with other protest activity such as machine breaking, striking or political protest.[95] In other views, food rioting was about to merge into a more generalised 'collective bargaining by riot' or alternatively was to be superseded by other forms of activity more appropriate to industrialised society.[96] In France, too, it has been argued, growing political participation for the masses and the organisation of an efficient market mechanism spelled the end of the food riot with the achievement of 'political and economic integration'.[97]

In December 1838 cartloads of potatoes were seized in Whitehaven market and sold at 4*d* per pound in the old style of former years, but such activities were becoming rarer.[98] There would be food riots in Cornwall as late as 1847, in the Scottish Highlands in the 1850s, and the last food riot in British history is still perhaps awaiting discovery, but the trend was towards other forms of action.[99] Food-rioting crowds in April 1812 in Lancashire and Cheshire were already rounding off their day with attacks upon mills which housed power-looms, and in August 1842, when provision shops were extensively entered in Manchester and food seized, this was no more than a subsidiary part of that complicated piece of industrial protest with political overtones, the Plug Plot. If food rioting was disappearing and giving way to other forms of protest, women, who were so prominently involved in food rioting, must themselves either disappear from the scene of protest or adapt to new techniques and discover other ways of making their presence felt.

3 WOMEN IN SOCIAL PROTEST

Food rioting was the main form of social protest with which women were identified in the first half of the nineteenth century. It was also an important feature of the background against which Luddism, or machine breaking, took place in 1811 – 12 in its three principal centres, Nottingham, Leeds and Manchester, all of which had major food riots apparently led by women. The machine breaking of the south Lancashire cotton area, where steam looms were the target of the rioters, was less precisely organised than in the hosiery and woollen districts, and the assaults that occurred on mills might well be the climax of a day of food rioting. The attack on Burton's Mill at Middleton on 20 April was in part a sequel to food riots in Oldham as colliers from Hollinwood and other rioters from Saddleworth marched from Oldham to Middleton and joined local crowds to attack Burton's power-loom factory.[1] The crowd at Middleton was said to have included a vast number of women and boys, armed principally with sticks, and a woman was subsequently charged with 'heading up' the party who set fire to furniture belonging to workers at the factory. In fact the Treasury Solicitor's Office subsequently prepared cases against five women for their part in the Middleton riots, extending over 20 – 21 April. They were Anne Dean, Alice Partington (a married woman) and four single persons, two named Ann Butterworth, Millicent Stoddart and Anne Dean. All were charged with rioting and accused of creating 'noise and tumult' and breaking the windows of Burton's Mill as well as being part of another crowd at a private house which broke windows, twelve chairs, five tables and fifty pieces of earthenware, for which they each received sentences of six months' imprisonment.[2] Two other women who became drawn into Luddism were the Molyneux sisters, Mary, aged 19, and Lydia, aged 15, who could so easily have been executed for their part in the attack upon West Houghton Mill on 24 April. These young women behaved dramatically and prominently and virtually ensured their recognition and arrest. They were seen 'with muck hooks and Coal Picks in their Hands, breaking the Windows of the Buildings and swearing and cursing the souls of those that worked in the Factory': Mary was heard to cry out 'set Fire to it', and when men got into

47

the buildings both the women clapped their hands and were heard to shout 'Now Lads'. For such offences the prosecuting counsel was advised to stress the need for speedy punishment and the court's duty to punish wrongdoers.[3] Despite the evidence against them the two women were acquitted, saved in part by their sex.[4]

This rioting and the encouragement of crowds were probably the limit of female involvement in the organisational side of Lancashire Luddism, which was weak anyway. Women were readily caught up in crowds which expressed popular fury against an institution, the steam loom, that was supposedly responsible for the current economic plight of weavers, though there is no evidence that they were involved in any planned attacks on machinery. Indeed, there is very little evidence that any of the Lancashire attacks were pre-planned.

On the basis of this kind of female activity it would be wrong to attribute very clear motive and intent to Lancashire female Luddites in 1812. In 1779 there had been extensive female participation in Jenny riots, which destroyed the new spinning machines together with other machinery for the spinning of yarn.[5] The threat of the Jenny had been clear. Now the steam loom served more as a convenient target for popular hostility than as an actual threat to women's jobs, and it is mistaken to suppose that women's objections were equally clear on the two occasions. In the context of new technology threatening existing jobs, the anti-steam-loom riots of 1826 make more sense, but women's greater participation in this year is also more ironical since it was the power looms that were about to enhance women's role within the factory population. In riots at Blackburn, a crowd consisting chiefly of women and boys was said to have performed little mischief beyond the breaking of a few windows, though Mary Simpson, a weaver's wife, was shot dead through the left thigh.[6] By the time of the Lancashire Assizes other women had been more fully involved in the actual mill attacks, and Betty Haworth, Mary Hindle, Anne Entwistle, Mary Marsden, Margaret Yates, Betty Cunliffe and Ann Ingham were all capitally convicted of riotously breaking into mills and destroying looms. Two of these women were actually transported for their offences, though none was executed.[7]

On the whole machine breaking appears to have been men's work, and there is no evidence that women formed part of the organised gangs of stockingers, lace-workers or croppers who created much havoc in the East Midlands by destroying stocking or lace frames, and the West Riding through the destruction of shearing frames and gig mills. The Special Commission which was held at York at the beginning of 1813 to try cases arising out of the late disturbances in Yorkshire was concerned only with male offenders. Earlier Mary Gibbons had been given a year's imprisonment for her part in attacking the military depot at Sheffield in April 1812, in what was an extension of food rioting in that city,[8] but she would be hard to classify as a Luddite despite the readiness of contemporaries to put into one category all the different people who were disturbing the peace of society in different ways, and men were the only Luddites who were caught and tried in the hosiery counties. The women of the troubled districts doubtless contributed a lot to the community backing and protection that the Luddites received, but their role was probably described accurately by Frank Peel in his imaginative account, written in 1880, in which the wives waited anxiously at home for the return of their husbands from their dangerous and illegal nocturnal missions.[9] There were features of Luddite enterprise, shared by many of the later Swing riots, which made them unsuitable for women's participation, and these will be considered later.

In the East Anglian riots of 1816 one woman, Mary Jackson, was arrested in a group of eight for her part in the ceremonious destruction of a threshing machine; this was no secret enterprise but rather an open, public exhibition, devised as such.[10]

Machine breaking, particularly the destruction of threshing machines, was the biggest category of incident associated with the Swing riots of 1830 – 1, but women appear to have played no great part in either the machine breaking or the labourers' riots as a whole. It has been suggested that had prices risen more steeply at the time of the riots women's involvement would have been much higher.[11] As it was, only 22 women were arrested and charged, usually with arson or the writing of threatening letters, and only 5 with the crime of machine breaking. Of the seven tried for arson two were convicted: Sarah Wheeler, who was imprisoned for a year, and Elizabeth Studham, who was transported to Tasmania after having been convicted of setting fire to the outbuildings of Birchington workhouse near Maidstone. The latter was 'supposed to be of loose habits' and committed further offences in the colony, being tried for theft on two occasions.[12] The only other woman to be transported after the Swing riots was Elizabeth Parker, who found herself for a time the lone female in a group of 82 prisoners in Gloucester gaol.[13] Her crimes were many. After receiving a seven-year sentence for 'breaking and destroying a threshing machine valued £50, the property of Jacob Hayward', she was reprieved but received a subsequent life sentence for larceny. She admitted having been 'on the town' for two and half years before being transported and was convicted of eighteen further offences in the colony, including drunkenness, indecent exposure, and being in bed in a bawdy house after hours.[14] Although caught up in social protest movements, she appears to have been something less than ideal for a female counterpart of the 'village Hampdens'.

If repression took little of a toll upon female participants in the labourers' riots of 1830 – 1, this is principally because they played an insignificant part in these movements. Inevitably women appeared in some crowds; on 22 November, for example, 'a riotous mob', said to consist of the 'lowest class of poor', the great part of whom were young men and women, rioted at Hungerford, demanding wage increases. About 170 panes of glass were broken on this occasion, and there is temptation to regard this as fairly characteristic women's protest.[15] Women were also said to be prominent in another wage riot at Leckford in the same month.[16] But despite these occasional mentions, the remarkable thing about hundreds of accounts of riots that were sent to the Home Office is the paucity of such references, the fact that in the overwhelming majority of cases women received no mention at all.

The relationship of the Swing riots to local price movements is doubtless of importance in explaining the relative passivity of women in this movement, but it is possible to offer further suggestions why Swing, to the extent that it was both the work of itinerant groups and in part a night-time operation, did not have much direct participation from women. When activities and incidents arose during daylight hours when women were going about their routine communal activities, such as shopping in the market-place or the town-centre, they would be much more likely to be drawn into popular protest, even as leaders, than at other times; and especially would they be drawn into food riots. If protest was less spontaneous and more organised, women would be less likely to become involved. Although they might themselves rally crowds in public places, they do not appear to have been themselves recruited into the organised parties that planned, plotted, and carried out secret activities. It seems unlikely that machine breaking was planned in a leisure situation where men and women got together to discuss concerted action, for such opportunites for discussion were minimal. It is more probable that, in the absence of women, male conspirators came together at the local pub or their place of work to plot destruction from which women were almost inevitably excluded. Lancashire Luddism had shown that where there was a large element of spontaneity women were involved; where it was highly organised, pre-planned and secret, as in Nottinghamshire and the West Riding, they were not. When it was a question of night work, whether in the service of General Ludd or Captain Swing, women were likely to be in their beds or at least at home with their children; women were diurnal social protestors. When masks had to be donned, faces blackened and heavy hammers swung, this was not women's work and women seem to have played little or no part in it. This was almost as true of the breaking of agricultural machinery as it was of stocking frames or shearing frames.

More closely related to those matters of domestic economy that were presumed to be the women's province was the issue of enclosure. Although enclosure was for a long time taken for granted as a principal cause of rural discontent in the late eighteenth and early nineteenth centuries, attempts to demonstrate its capacity to produce riot and disturbance on a wide scale have not been very successful. The causal links between enclosure, discontent and disturbance are easier to assume than to demonstrate. There are nevertheless several notable occasions on which anti-enclosure protest clearly occurred, and women did make a contribution to these incidents. They seem to have happened most frequently in Wales. In 1793 a case had occurred in Flint in which a man, imprisoned and charged with pulling down a fence, was released by a crowd which celebrated its success by pulling down and burning more fences on its return home. Ann Jones, a widow of Caergwrle, had helped to supervise the work of destruction just as she had helped to feed and entertain the rioters in the evening.[17] There were further incidents in 1809, when women were taken into custody during riots at St Clears for pulling down fences, and again in 1812, when two female rioters, Margaret Rowland and Anne Humphrey, were sentenced to six months' imprisonment for their part in an attack on magistrates and constables who were pelted with sods of earth. This treatment was mild compared with the assault upon enclosure officials by women, armed with dripping pans, who descended 'like a rolling torrent'. And this was exceeded in sheer menace by the crowd of Cardiganshire women who, in 1820, dug a pit for the interment of every surveyor who invaded their rights. The preservation of land rights was clearly an issue central to women's role in safeguarding the home and family against the forces that threatened them, particularly if they happened to be Welsh homes and families threatened by English exploitation. The authorities often complained that they had more trouble with the women than with the men, and that, far from being a restraining influence upon men during these incidents, they tended to be in the forefront of the crowds, driving the men on with their taunts and provocation.[18]

English women by contrast had a less impressive record of resistance on this kind of issue, though in April 1815, Anne Rush was indicted along with three men for wilfully and maliciously damaging a fence after the Lopham Enclosure Act had been passed.[19] Significantly enough, the other setting for extensive women's participation in riots relating to the land question was elsewhere within the 'Celtic fringes'.

Long before the time of the Highland Clearances, women of the northern Scottish counties had established a leadership of popular resistance to the imposition of unpopular ministers by the local landlord. In the early years of the eighteenth century, the Lord Advocate received an account of troubles at Dingwall:

> The Minister of Dingwall dying anno 1704 and buryed on a Fryday the verie next Sabbath Fowlis [Sir Robert Munro of Fowlis, a leading Whig and Presbyterian] and his presbyterian Minister with three or four score of men armed, came to the Town, broke open the Church doors and sett a guard thereupon. The Magistrates of the Village being near two miles out of town in the next adjacent church, at sermon, and that the whole town being of episcopal persuasion, the women and the servants [i.e. women servants] did raise a mobb, and chased the Minister with Fowlis and his armed men out of the town, with little or no hurt, only two or three women of the town being wounded at the beginning which was what incensed the mobb the more. This matter was judged by the Sherriff and both parties figned as illegal actors.[20]

The Easter Ross disturbances of the early century were complemented by late-century outbreaks of a similar kind in

Sutherland, when women were hurt in the parish of Assynt after a crowd of them had blocked church doors by piling stones against them, following the presentation of an unacceptable minister.[21]

More dramatic, more widespread, and by far the most aggressive female activity in early-nineteenth-century social protest is to be found in the Highland Clearance riots, which have been described as being, to a remarkable degree, women's riots.[22] These episodes were accompanied by sporadic food riots in which women protested against potato and grain prices in Caithness and Ross by urging on their menfolk or by actively rioting themselves. As they did in other isolated rural areas, such as Cornwall, food riots persisted in the north of Scotland when they had been superseded by other forms of protest in the industrial centres; in February, 1846, for example, an estimated crowd of 5,000, led by a screaming woman standing in a cart, unloaded a convoy of potatoes in traditional style and battled for two days with special constables.[23] But there was far more at stake than food prices and food shortages in the Highlands, as absentee landowners, through their agents, attempted to transform the Highland economy and society by evicting and clearing their tenants and replacing them by sheep. There were large numbers of evictions in Sutherland, Ross, Argyll, Inverness and the Hebrides in the period 1811 – 20, and a second major wave of clearances occurred in the late 1840s and early 1850s as the cost of pauper relief mounted in the wake of the potato blight that struck the crofters' staple diet.[24] Evictions were a threat to a whole way of life. The need to defend the home, the family and the land, which had an almost sacred quality in Scottish peasant culture, inspired feats of heroism amongst the women, who were always in the forefront of the resistance, which was spontaneous and non-political in its nature, sporadic in its occurrence, and devoted to a conservative, not to say reactionary, social and economic ideal that was under threat. The big landowners and their agents were the authors of the threat, but it was the sheriffs' officers, the constables and the soldiers who delivered and implemented it and it was they who felt the force of women's resistance, which surpassed that of the men both in its determination and in its violence.

In the general protest technique found in a large number of clearance riots, women formed the front line of defence, making the most determined stand and often bearing the worst injuries. The men formed a second force used to support their women, or were dressed as women in the front line. In 1820 female rioters in Ross-shire clashed with the attacking military force, and when a young girl was shot, the young men concealed close by then attacked the soldiers and forced their retreat.[25] At Coigeach, it was the women who disarmed twenty constables and sheriff's officers, burned the summonses, and threw their opponents' batons into the sea prior to ducking their owners, while the male crofters did not touch the officers of the law, merely being present in case the women could not cope.[26] At Greenyards in Ross-shire in 1853, the sheriff's officers and 30 constables were met by a crowd of 300 crofters. Two-thirds were women, who lined up in front with weapons of sticks and stones, and who sustained the worst injuries in the short, bloody struggle.[27] Fifteen to 20 women were seriously injured by police brutality, and the *Inverness Courier* reported an interesting aspect; when the constables attacked, the men ran and left the women to fight instead of supporting their struggles as at Coigeach and Culrain. Either discretion was the better part of valour, or the men regarded the women as being capable of looking after themselves. However, as in all struggles, the result was defeat for the crofters; when the women eventually fled up the brae, the sheriff and constables executed their summonses.[28]

The apparent willingness of the male crofters to allow women a front-line defence position in clashes with authority must derive in part from a commonly accepted view that the issues at stake were traditionally women's concerns. There is also evidence of an assumption that the rioters' femininity brought them a certain immediate advantage, which is supported by the element of transvestism in the riots. An interesting case occurred at Glencarvie in 1843. Women led the attack as at Coigeach, and, following the Greenyards skirmish, four women were arrested for being 'ringleaders in the riot and mobbing'.[29] The advantage of this tactic appears in the authorities' dogged relief that riot ringleaders should be male; only one of these women was later charged, while the messenger-at-arms in nearby Tain returned with two policemen to arrest the allegedly true ringleader, of necessity a man. Thus Peter Ross, who, if present, played only a minor role in the Greenyards incident, was taken into custody and the authorities were temporarily satisfied.[30]

It would also be relevant to note that the Highland women were used to an arduous role and that they were accustomed to working beside their menfolk performing strenuous duties in general farming. They were unaccustomed to a privileged role and would not have expected to take a back seat in defence of their way of life. They were also themselves the frequent victims of brutal evictions, if Alexander Mackenzie is to be believed. Henny Munro, an aged infirm widow, for example, denied help to move her furniture, was forced to remove all her belongings by herself only minutes before her cottage was fired, and she later collapsed from her exertions.[31] Such incidents doubtless roused the blood of other women and helped to inspire the heroism of the women of Culrain in March 1820. The *Black Dwarf* reported:

> The mob appeared as if raving mad; and those who first attacked seemed furious, and were chiefly women. The men were drawn up on a height, and had taken quite a military position behind a wall, with their firearms in readiness . . . the women, instead of running away, as expected, literally rushed among the bayonets.

Afterwards they supposedly cried: 'We must die anyway, better to die here than in America or the Cape of Good Hope; we don't care for our lives,' an outburst indicative of the sort of emotions aroused by their predicament.[32]

The supposed advantages and immunities of female rioters, in the Highlands and elsewhere, merit further consideration. Undoubtedly the authorities were inclined to underestimate the rioting capacity of women in their search for specifically male ringleaders, and the crofters did take advantage of their indecision. At the same time the quoted remark of the Sutherland agent in 1821 that 'The opinion of the people here is that they [the women] can do anything with impunity' indicates an attitude some way removed from realism and one likely to inspire reckless conduct.[33] When two women and three men were convicted of obstructing an eviction officer in Caithness, they all received identical sentences of six months' imprisonment, and other evidence on this issue is too patchy to permit any conclusions being drawn with confidence.[34] On this subject the most frequently quoted statement is that of Robert Southey, in 1809, who wrote:

> Women are more disposed to be mutinous, they stand less in fear of the law partly from ignorance, partly because they presume upon the privilege of their sex, and therefore in all public

tumults   they   are   foremost   in   violence   and   ferocity.[35]

Some belief in immunity from arrest and lighter penalties probably did exist, and sometimes this confidence was justified. Constables did sometimes hesitate to arrest women, and sometimes the sex of the offender allowed women to escape with mitigated punishments. But expectations of such leniency were a very dubious basis on which to act, for there was no predictable or consistent response from the authorities. Anne Catherall and Elizabeth Huxley of Hawarden, Flintshire, were sentenced to seven years' transportation in 1796 for unloading bags of wheat from a wagon for resale in the market, a penalty sufficiently stringent to do nothing 'pour encourager les autres'.[36] And cases have already been noted of the severe penalties inflicted upon a Manchester food-rioting woman in 1812 and the East Anglian rioters of 1816, two of whom were transported whilst others probably thought themselves lucky to escape so lightly with sentences of hard labour when Australia beckoned. In 1826 there were seven capital convictions of women for the Lancashire mill attacks and the breaking of steam looms in that year, and, though no woman was executed, two were transported. These penalties suggest that it was a mistake to have confidence in any feminine advantage before the law, for severe retribution was a likely consequence of conviction, whatever the initial advantages women might have had in escaping apprehension by overwhelming or outmanoeuvring Riot Act-reading magistrates or conscientious constables.

At the same time it must be recognised that there were occasions when women were saved, or at least treated more lightly, because of their sex. The Molyneux sisters, for instance, the wielders of 'Muck hooks and Coal Picks' against West Houghton mill were discharged, though the Crown had an impressive list of witnesses and convincing case against them. Four men, some but not all of whom were more directly involved in the breaking of machinery, were hanged for their part in the attack. At Middleton too five women who could well have received much more severe punishments received prison sentences of six months, the same as a man similarly convicted; in the words of the Hammonds, this was a 'light punishment'.[37] During the renewed machine breaking in Lancashire in 1826 seven women were capitally convicted and two transported but none was hanged. The men convicted on the same charges were similarly treated, and no machine breakers were hanged for outbreaks which were more extensive in Lancashire than those of 1812. During the Swing riots the number of convicted women was very small, but so too was the number of participating women, and by the time of the Anti-Poor Laws riots the authorities were more disposed to arrest and release than to prosecute. The evidence for supposing that female offenders enjoyed immunities and advantages is far from conclusive. They probably found it easier to escape arrest, but once within the clutches of the law they were subject to the same whims and arbitrary conduct that decided the fate of men.

Despite this, there seems little doubt that matters relating to the domestic economy and the home, food prices, enclosures, evictions and the like were deemed an appropriate area for women's concern and provoked a considerable amount of social protest well before any campaign for political rights or other aspects of female emancipation. Although it would be wrong to claim these areas as an exclusively female domain, it is important to remember the frequent complaints that female food or enclosure rioters were the worst troublemakers, that women often failed to restrain their menfolk, and that they were evidently making a sufficient social impact to have their role identified and deplored. Wielding sticks, stones, pans or whatever came to hand, and employing coarse expressive language, women terrified many official opponents and placed themselves in the forefront of economic protest. In mixed crowds they frequently demonstrated an ability to take control of the situation and revealed a strength of purpose, initiative and power seemingly at odds with the typically subservient Victorian women. The preservation of life and living standards roused them to heights of unfeminine verbal and physical violence, sometimes on their own, sometimes with men, and occasionally alongside men who were legitimising their rights to protest in particular areas by dressing as women. Within these areas the presence of women provided a unifying element in otherwise geographically and thematically diverse movements, and they were on occasions a determined force to be reckoned with in early-nineteenth-century British society, at least for those who had the immediate task of confronting them. Their lack of any general recognition presumably arises from the fact that their successes were too limited geographically and too restricted in time to make any general, long-term impact upon the social or economic system, even if their aims had been so ambitious as this. Stunned opponents might be rendered temporarily inactive and short-term advantages could be exploited, but their overall impact was minimal. It would require action of a different kind to change society, and women of a different outlook. They were soon to appear.

The turning-point for women's social protest, in England at least, was the campaign against the New Poor Law of 1834, for this movement was the bridge between older forms of direct action, involving violence, and newer forms of political organisation and the use of political techniques. The protest against the Poor Law had both elements in abundance, but by the time the anti-Poor Law movement had merged into Chartism many women were thoroughly involved in political processes, and the days of physical confrontation with the forces of law and order were coming to an end. The female anti-Poor Law associations led directly to the female Radical and Chartist associations, and the campaign for the abolition of the New Poor Law became a more generalised campaign for working-class political rights through Chartism.

The early reactions and responses to the Poor Law were mild and sporadic compared with the later crescendo of protest. In August 1834 a letter appeared in *The Times* from 'An Englishwoman', attacking in particular the new bastardy clause which threatened to make the mother entirely responsible for the upkeep of her illegitimate child; by focusing on the issue of motherhood, the anonymous writer legitimised her right to involve herself in this political question, and validity and acceptance were accorded to women's participation in protest because of their social role as mothers.[38] The *Poor Man's Guardian* supported its stand on this issue on the grounds that 'woman the weaker vessel' needed the more protection, being a creature of 'affection, sincerity, softness, and constancy'.[39] And the women's leaders themselves were not averse to employing 'sexist' arguments to justify their opposition to the new law as well as their right to act upon their opposition. Women, said Mary Grassby of Elland, who might have been accorded a higher status in women's history if she had been more reluctant to employ this kind of argument, had more need to oppose the New Poor Law because they had more to fear from it than had men; the break-up of the family, which the workhouse entailed, would be a bigger blow for women than for men, since their feelings were more susceptible.[40] She can be defended on the grounds that, if she wanted her arguments to be heard at all within a male-dominated society, she had to use whatever means were available to her, and perhaps these were the only means to ensure any kind of sympathetic response.

The New Poor Law threatened a radical disturbance of the family unit by separating husbands and wives and removing children, and by moving the relieved poor from the home to the workhouse, thus giving women the most socially acceptable and morally unimpeachable cause on which to fight, the defence of the family; this led them naturally to a whole host of Biblical texts and religious quotations to justify an unwomanly political crusade. It was a radical disturbance by the central government of a long-established familiar pattern of provincial life in which the poor were treated within the community by locally responsible people. But it was also a severe assault upon working-class security, threatening to punish the poverty and unemployment that were endemic within working-class society, a piece of class legislation which could be resisted, eventually, only by political rights and political power in the hands of people who saw themselves oppressed by the 1834 Act. Politics eventually became necessary because the Poor Law was in essence a political question. Protest became necessarily political and of necessity radical.

This did not mean that the transition was either sudden or comprehensive, for direct and political action coexisted at least throughout 1838. After some years of passive resistance to the new Act of 1834, in the industrial north and Midlands, administrators, officials and Guardians found themselves subject to a large measure of violence as attempts to implement the law eventually got under way. Assistant Commissioner Alfred Power was assaulted in Bradford and Keighley,[41] and in Elland, in February 1838, a party of women, having been thwarted in their attempts to disrupt a meeting of Assistant Commissioners, took their revenge by rolling the Guardians in the snow, despite the offer of bribes of ale.[42] This was an act of greater social significance than the reported case of Sarah Gill, who had been charged, the previous month, with lurching at the gates of Holborn Workhouse and creating a disturbance.[43] Bigger disturbances occurred in the Dewsbury riots of August. For the second time, a meeting of Guardians late in the month was the cause of rioting in the town, during which women were very prominent, uttering cries of 'Go it, lads', 'Down with 'em,' 'D — n that Ingham,' and 'Murder them London ——.' Stones allegedly began to fly like hail, directed away from windows and entirely towards persons. The leading protestor was Mary Hay, thought to be between 40 and 50 years of age, who was repeatedly warned to leave the street but continued to throw stones herself and to urge others to 'go it,' showing no subsequent sign of contrition for her performance but rather seeming to rejoice over an exhibition in which she had sketched her own possible future in the Bastille and her resolve to be mistress. Wisely the authorities chose to discharge her rather than risk making her a martyr.[44]

In November 1838, Todmorden on the Yorkshire/Lancashire border was also the scene of two outbursts of rioting against the Poor Law. On the first occasion 'when the woman rang the handbell, the factory bells began to ring, and the work people left their work' and began to assemble. The female bell-ringer is almost a classic figure in events of this kind. The house of a Guardian was surrounded by a multitude of 'many hundreds of persons of both sexes' and two officers from Halifax were 'outrageously assaulted' by the rioters.[45]

Not all such incidents occurred in the north. On 11 October, it was reported, a crowd of almost 100 women stole a cartload of bread marked for distribution amongst paupers in Combe St Nicholas, Dorset, in protest against the withdrawal of outdoor relief to the able-bodied poor. After pummelling the baker's boy who was driving the cart, the riotous women, emboldened with beer and gin from a nearby inn, threatened to duck the relieving officer and 'deprive him of his life before he got home'. Afterwards they were to be observed 'regaling themselves in the streets with tea'.[46]

The most serious and largest-scale of all anti-Poor Law demonstrations was the attack on Carmarthen Workhouse in June 1843, when the male Rebeccaites turned their attention temporarily away from toll-gates and towards another unpopular institution. On this occasion a large gathering of Rebeccaites and Chartist demonstrators preceded by a band was accompanied by a crowd of women, many of whom carried brooms with which they declared their intention to sweep away the foundations of the workhouse, a nice touch of symbolism to extend the domestic cleaning role into a more public theatre. An orgy of destruction was stopped short of general conflagration by the arrival of a military force, which made about 100 arrests. Of those captured, the women were set free, a not unusual occurrence, possibly made more likely in a geographical context where men were so ready to play the woman's part, though one woman, Francis Evans, had played too prominent a role to be ignored. At the subsequent trials she was charged with having incited and led the mob in their riotous attack; she had been seen leading people up some stairs and later 'dancing with violent gestures on the table in the hall'.[47] This doughty demonstrator appears to belong to the long tradition of female rebels who supplied an extra flamboyancy and panache to set the seal on their performance.

She was far removed from the women of Yorkshire who organised 'Oastler Festivals' in 1841. When the Factory King had been dismissed from his stewardship at Fixby Hall in August 1838, crowds had demonstrated on his behalf, including 'ladies' who showed their disapprobation of the act of dismissal by waving a flag condemning the bastardy clause of the Poor Law.[48] These 'ladies' were to the fore in organising the Oastler Festivals of January 1841. The *Leeds Intelligencer* chose to pick out the fact that tea was served by the ladies' committee on these occasions; the women of Bradford were said to be 'conspicuous for their neatness and elegance of their dress'; of those from Huddersfield their 'attention to comfort and cleanliness deserves high commendation'.[49] This patronising reporting is rather more than male indulgence in attitudes of *noblesse oblige*; it is more a deliberate focusing on activity that fitted the social stereotype at a time when the whole anti-Poor Law protest had turned many women towards political organisation and away from the purely auxiliary, tea-serving role that men might well have preferred.

In the early months of 1838 there sprang up a great number of active female anti-Poor Law societies throughout Yorkshire, Lancashire, Cheshire and the more northerly counties. That at Elland, led by the formidable trio of Mary Grassby, Susannah Fearnley and Elizabeth Hansen, appears to have been the prototype and the trend-setter,[50] but others were founded in Bradford, Dewsbury, Huddersfield, Liversedge, Barnsley, Hyde, Stalybridge, Middleton, Manchester, Wigton and Carlisle, and probably many other places. Figures are almost non-existent for the membership of these associations, but it is evident that many of them held frequent meetings of large numbers of women and that women became more accustomed to airing their grievances, speaking in public and involving themselves in a whole range of political activities than ever before. The number of organisations far exceeded that of the female reform societies of 1819 and was in turn greatly exceeded by the number of female Chartist associations that were to develop out of the anti-Poor Law movement.

Their activities and techniques were various. In some places women were at first evident in their mass attendance at men's meetings, bodies like the 'large number of females occupying the gallery' at a Barnsley meeting in February 1838, which helped inspire the editor of the *Northern Star* to address the 'Glorious men, women and children' of the movement.[51] Soon women were organising and chairing their own weekly meetings and providing their own speakers, though star attractions from outside, such as O'Connor or Stephens, continued to address the big demonstrations. At these women would attend in well organised groups bearing their own banners suitably inscribed. At a radical demonstration at Carlisle in October 1838, 366 women were reported to have taken part, carrying a silk flag depicting a Poor Law Guardian tearing a child away from the mother and, on its reverse side, a Guardian separating a man and wife, with the familiar motto subscribed:'Whom God has joined together let no man put asunder.'[52] Women from Colne and Marsden carried similar banners in another demonstration earlier in the month at Colne.[53] On occasions female speakers resorted to dramatic rhetoric not far short of that delivered by the fiery male orators of Chartism, describing their campaign as a glorious battle for liberty or a threatened civil war; the women of Carlisle promised O'Connor that they would

> follow our husbands, our fathers, our sons, and our brothers, to the battlefield, to cheer and comfort them in the hour of danger, bind up their wounds, and instigate them to fresh deeds of valour, and if we perish in the attempt, we shall account our death a thousand times more desirable . . . than that of perishing in a miserable Whig bastille.[54]

The women of Elland were even urged to take the law into their own hands, a rare declaration of the resolution of women to act independently of their menfolk in a political struggle.[55] These threats and promises, like so many made by male Chartist leaders, proved in the event to be little more than threats and promises.

More common were the pledges to give full support to anything that the men should undertake in the anti-Poor Law movement, the signing of women's petitions to the government and the Queen, or co-operation in a joint petitioning movement with the men. In the early days there was some uncertainty about the part that women should play in signing petitions. At a large delegate meeting in Manchester on 5 February 1838, members brought petitions from their various towns; Mr Taylor of Leeds brought two, one of 1,065 signatures 'besides a petition signed by 254 females'.

> On the mention of this last petition, a question arose as to whether females were allowed to sign petitions: all the delegates were of opinion that had they had their petitions signed by females the signatures would have been increased fourfold. One gentleman stated that in the Macclesfield union they had two females as guardians (loud cheers). It was then unanimously decided that it would be better to get up a number of petitions signed exclusively by females.[56]

Whether this was a victory or a defeat for women's rights is difficult to judge.

There must also be some question concerning the relationship between the female protestors and the Reverend J. R. Stephens, of a kind that had been raised by the mutual love affair between Henry Hunt and his female audiences and would later be raised by Henry Vincent. There were many emotional outbursts in March 1839 concerning the arrest and trial of Stephens, and numerous Female Societies demonstrated great fervour in pledging their support, both moral and financial, for campaigning for his release, and their faith in his actions.

The ideology of women's protest against the New Poor Law is something of a mixture of social conservatism and rationalisation on the one hand and the enunciation of radical political principles on the other. The need to explain their very involvement in politics inevitably threw women into a situation in which they felt obliged to emphasise their own role as mothers, within marriage and the family, so justifying their defence of traditional institutions under threat. To strengthen their case they stressed the offence to morality and decency contained within the workings of the Act, and they cited scriptural texts to show that it was contrary to the will of God. Their hymns, their prayers and their chapel meetings all served to strengthen this defence of their conduct by showing that morality and tradition were on their side. This willingness to resort to arguments about woman 'the weaker vessel' being more in need of protection against the Act should not, however, be allowed to obscure their readiness to argue on behalf of both a class interest and political principles as yet unestablished.

Condemnation of bastille diet, pauper labour and even the threat to the fabric of working-class life involved fairly obvious points that had to be made, but more sophisticated arguments were sometimes used. Mrs Grassby, in a nice mixture of working-class concern and Tory politics, said that the Act infringed working-class rights 'Because it takes all power out of the hands of those who pay and who have the best right of knowledge and means of disposing of the poor rates, because it places the sole power in the hands of these Commissioners who are utter strangers to the poor.'[57] Her colleague, Elizabeth Hansen, argued for a more egalitarian approach to the whole question of poverty and the maintenance of the poor by suggesting that the parklands and private estates of England could, if necessary, be ploughed up to grow more corn for poor people to eat.[58] The Queen, or Chief Magistrate of the Country, being a woman, must surely, it was supposed, share their concerns and support their right to do something about them.[59] There is little evidence to suggest that their campaigns met with her approval, though there were plenty of indications of male support for what the women were trying to do. Against this must be balanced the scorn and contempt that women expected to encounter, as well as the accusations and innuendoes about their private lives. Still, on balance, the anti-Poor Law movement must be considered a notable step forward by women into the men's world of politics.

4 WOMEN IN INDUSTRIAL PROTEST

The friendly societies of the eighteenth and nineteenth centuries were defensive institutions of self-protection rather than aggressive ones of protest, yet they did have some part to play in the developing capacity of women to organise themselves and to respond to their economic situation. Though not trade unions in composition or in function, they were sometimes a cover for quasi-trade union activities during the period of the Combination Laws, 1799 – 1824, and in Edward Thompson's view constituted a working-class subculture out of which the less stable unions of the early nineteenth century were to grow.[1] By the start of the nineteenth century they had probably around three-quarters of a million members of both sexes, some societies being exclusively female, and their members spread over all trade and occupational groups rather than being confined to one in particular.[2] Their main purpose was to help in the amelioration of poor living and working conditions by providing sickness, unemployment or funeral benefits to members in their times of greatest need; during periods of industrial unrest their funds might be utilised to support people on strike, which was not their intended purpose and not a matter for social approval.

Incidentally, they gave their members, men and women, valuable practice in leadership and decision-taking in democratically organised societies, providing a training or experience, akin to that which has frequently been attributed to Methodist chapels, to ordinary people, some of whom subsequently employed their talents in public or political life. Like the chapels, many of the female friendly societies sought to give moral guidance to their members and to censure them for their failings: the Birmingham Women's Benefit Society refused sickness benefits to members with venereal disease 'or any other disorder occasioned by a loose and vicious life'; North Shields denied benefits to mothers of illegitimate children and would not pay funeral expenses to cover suicides; the Wakefield Society imposed fines for drunkenness and disorderly behaviour.[3]

The friendly societies were not obsessively devoted to rooting out sin but were also concerned to entertain their members and make their own lives more enjoyable. In Wolverhampton regular dinners were held where women were initiated into the organisation prior to an evening of 'dancing, humour, and conviviality'.[4] In Bradford, the Friendly Society of the United Order of Golden Fleece in March 1838 'sat down to a most excellent dinner; after which the dance, the song and recitations following in quick succession passed away the evening merrily'.[5] Detailed statistics of women's friendly societies are not available, but it is clear that they were common organisations, and it seems certain that they must have brought pleasure into the lives of many working women and a measure of planning and rationality into domestic economies prosperous enough to afford the modest subscriptions required.

For these reasons they were a boon to working-class women, and for other reasons too, for they were the means by which many were able to effect at least a temporary escape from the pressures of home and share out some of their domestic responsibilities with their men. This was not an argument in their favour where polite society was concerned, and the association of the friendly societies with pubs and clubs helped to strengthen the popular prejudice that they were an undermining influence on the virtues that the women ought to possess, particularly sobriety and domesticity. The 1840 report on handloom weavers mentioned the temptations to which women were exposed in the pubs of Coventry through their membership of societies, and Lord Ashley regaled the House of Commons in 1844 with a story, subsequently much quoted, that was obviously intended to reinforce this stern warning.

> A man came into one of these club rooms, with a child in his arms. 'Come lass', said he, addressing one of the women, 'come home, for I cannot keep this bairn quiet, and the other I have left crying at home.' 'I won't go home, idle devil', she replied. 'I have thee to keep, and the bairns too, and if I can't have a pint of ale quietly it's too tiresome. This is only the second pint Bess and me have had between us; thou may sup if thou likes, and sit down, but I won't go home yet.'[6]

It might be suggested that the story could be otherwise intepreted; that the woman was enjoying her first taste of sexual equality; that in breaking free from her home for once and leaving her husband to mind the babies, she was emancipating herself and taking the first step towards activities of greater social and political significance than drinking in a public house. If the friendly societies themselves did not lead directly to trade unionism or some other organisation for industrial protest, they must at least have encouraged attitudes that would assist women towards such purposes if Lord Ashley's female villain was in any way characteristic of general membership.

It is not surprising that women had no great role to play in industrial protest; whereas male industrial labour expected to have to contend with the employers as the principal adversary, female labour faced both the employers and the men, who felt themselves threatened by women workers. They were widely viewed as cheap labour, threatening men's wages by their willingness to work at lower rates and appealing to employers for this reason and for their general tractability. Indeed, Andrew Ure had offered this as part of his *Philosophy of Manufactures*, that the constant aim of technological improvements was to supersede human labour and cut costs, which would be achieved 'by substituting the industry of women and children for that of men'.[7] This is not an appropriate matter for continuing mutual recriminations between the sexes or the apportioning of blame between men who sought to exclude women from job opportunities and women who offered cheap labour that undermined the men's position.[8] The sex war was a by-product of the economic situation, not a cause of it, and it is sufficient to recognise that women were, during the decades of the Industrial Revolution, a numerous body of unskilled, often casual, workers who were ready to accept badly paid jobs in factories, in their homes, or wherever else work was available, with few opportunities to enjoy the benefits of collective bargaining. And if a new perspective is still sought on this subject, it can be found in John Foster's quotation from the Northampton shoemaker of the 1870s who expressed his abhorrence of 'the detestable custom of compelling women to do men's labour', which somehow transcends the battle of the sexes by demonstrating compassion rather than jealousy.[9]

The battle did, none the less, exist and on occasion led to male harassment of women workers who seemed to pose a threat within male strongholds. In July 1832, for instance, male cotton spinners in Glasgow struck at one mill because the master employed women and refused to return to work until they had been discharged.[10] More generally the threat was in part the consequence of what E. P. Thompson calls 'the abrogation of paternalist legislation'.[11] With the repeal of the Elizabethan Statute of Artificers in 1813, the need for formal apprenticeship in traditional skilled crafts disappeared and the way was open for unapprenticed and unskilled people, including women, to create a 'dishonourable' level of trade.[12] By working long hours at low rates and ignoring craft restrictions, they undermined the position of the skilled artisan, and those most notoriously ready to work at any price were women. In 1833, for example, the Factory Commissioners were informed of employers in the Birmingham area who were making direct substitutions for men because they could get the cheaper labour of boys or women to do the work that men used to perform; when vacancies occurred women were rushing to fill them for a wage as low as 4s 6d per week, and they inevitably incurred the hostility of men for their part in this process.[13]

They also caused resentment by their effective domination of power-loom weaving, cutting off one possible means of salvation for that large group of displaced handworkers, the handloom weavers.[14] Technological redundancy and the operation of new machinery became battle areas between the sexes when they should, in the opinion of some, have been issues for working-class solidarity in the face of a common threat. The sex battles are still in fact being fought; the women's success in power-loom weaving has been interpreted as fair compensation for the loss incurred by women when spinning was taken over by men; it has even been suggested that the men who took over this traditional women's employment, heedless of the consequences for the women concerned, were appropriately punished by the undercutting rates of women in general.[15] This misplaced enthusiasm for projecting modern sex politics into past tragedies has helped to produce some curious history, such as that of the male stockingers who allegedly attempted to prevent modifications to some fabulous powered knitting machine which would have allowed its operation by women and boys.[16] Imagination has run riot; there were no powered stocking frames in 1812, let alone projected modifications which would have allowed these mythical machines to be used by women, who were, in any case, quite accustomed to operating the old frames, worked by the arms and legs of their users, who paid dearly for the physical effort involved. Talk of new inventions appears to have derived from those singularly ill-informed aristocrats, the Duke of Newcastle and Lord Byron, and not even they could conceive the application of steam power which occurred in the second half of the century.[17] There is one clear example of Luddite hostility to women, at Pentridge in Derbyshire, where the machine breakers evidently demanded their dismissal, along with unapprenticed labour, but there is little evidence of general antagonism.[18]

The reality of male hostility was bad enough. This arose in part from the occasionally declared opposition of women to the strikes of their men which would frequently in the short term throw the precariously balanced family economy into disarray. Their attitude has been sympathetically explained as the 'defensive militancy' of women whose main occupations were those of mother and home-maker and whose main investment was in the family, which was inevitably in conflict with the class group to which they and their husbands belonged.[19]

Female opposition was reported to the Derby Union strike of 1833. Loud complaints were said to have been made from some female hands that they had nothing whatever to do with the unions yet they had been deprived of their only means of earning their bread, and it is significant that when the strike collapsed in the late spring of 1834 it was the women workers who first returned to work in large numbers.[20] Indeed, women had a reputation, deserved or otherwise, for continuing to work during strikes and for supplying a ready source of blackleg labour with which striking males could be supplanted. This kind of suspicion led to several outbursts of violence against women, which can easily be understood in the light of a report in *The Times* of December 1800. This deplored the fact that the tailors were in combination but welcomed the opportunity that was being provided to bring women into the trade to work at lower rates.[21]

Not surprisingly, violence against women sometimes accompanied 'turn-outs' by male workers or mixed bodies. During the Stockport power-loom weavers' strike of 1818, girls who wished to return to work had to be forcibly restrained from doing so by being held under a water pump.[22]

In 1824 six female spinners employed at Kelly's mill in the Glasgow district were threatened with frightful consequences if they remained in their employment, and discretion proved the better part of valour.[23] Glasgow featured in many such incidents. In July 1832 male cotton spinners struck against a master who employed women, refusing to return until the women were dismissed and threatening personal injury to the women as part of their campaign.[24] But it was the 1837 Glasgow cotton strike that produced the greatest number of actual physical assaults on women, including the murder of the mother of an accused blackleg and the notorious vitriol attack upon Mary M'Shaffrey, who had the misfortune to look like another woman who was supposed to be performing blackleg labour.[25] Such attacks, much publicised, could have given women in industry little zest for the strikes of the men and little enthusisasm for independent trade union organisation of their own.

Nor did the men offer much encouragement to women workers to participate in their unions, which were sometimes overtly hostile to women. In 1769, the Spitalfields silk weavers excluded women from the higher-paid work, and in 1779 the journeymen bookbinders excluded women from their union.[26] The Stockport Hat Makers' Society laid down rules and orders in 1808 which stated that all women were to be struck against, one shop at a time, until all the women in the trade had been removed.[27] In other well known instances, the women who had received equal strike pay during the Lancashire spinners' strike of 1818 were excluded from the union immediately afterwards for allegedly failing to observe trade union conditions;[28] and the cotton spinners' union of 1829 specifically excluded women.

Under article 24 of their rules women were to be no part of the General Union; no women mule spinners were to join the union and no more women were to be allowed to become mule spinners.[29] Women were seen to be taking jobs away from men, the interests of the sexes were believed to be in conflict, and in consequence women were discouraged, even deterred, from taking part with men in their union struggles and parliamentary campaigns. Although urged to form their own unions, the women were slow to do so, and conflict and competition, rather than co-operation, between the sexes were reinforced in the pattern of industrial relations.[30] Similarly in weaving, the handloom weavers, the biggest single group of textile workers, consistently refused to admit women to their unions, though this did little to avert their own eventual near extinction. Nor did it stop women working as handloom weavers as well as dominating power-loom weaving.

By the late 1820s, it has been suggested, the traditional practices of some old crafts of excluding women from guild membership on grounds of sex alone had generally been transferred to trade unionism.[31] In 1834 male London tailors struck work to drive women from their trade and to protect their standards; in 1844 the Sheffield file trade attempted, in vain, to exclude women, but they were forced out of ribbon factories, and acted against by the Potters' Union in 1845 over their working of new machinery.[32] If the working classes remained fragmented by occupation and skill in trade union organisation, they also remained divided by sex.

Apart from male opposition, there are two other principal reasons why women's industrial organisation made little headway in the first half of the nineteenth century. The first is the nature of women's work. Trade unions, in so far as they existed at this time, were for the skilled workers and the apprenticed tradesmen, and women rarely fell into these categories. On the whole they performed the subsidiary and unskilled tasks of their industries, where they belonged to industrial operations, and the textile, metal or pottery trades, for instance, left them for a long time in subordinate roles, performing unskilled or casual roles, probably the first to be semi- or unemployed during slack periods. Their dispersal in what were later to be termed 'the sweated trades', their widespread employment in agricultural tasks, and, above all, their involvement in that great consumer of female labour, domestic service, all contributed to removing women from situations where effective trade union organisation was easily possible, even if thought desirable. The Edinburgh Maidservants' Union Society of 1825, the Grand United Lodge of Operative Ladies' Maids of 1834, supplemented even by the organisation of Kensington Washer-women who struck in the same year, though interesting curiosities, must not be allowed to detract from the weakening effects of domestic service on women's capacity to organise as a labour force in the nineteenth century.[33]

The other great inhibiting factor was the existing social stereo-type, the woman whose place was in the home. When women were performing a great variety of laborious, physically demanding duties they were idealised as delicate and gentle; at the same time as the processes of industrialisation were summoning them forth from their homes, they were repeatedly being told that this was in fact where they ought to remain. The social evils attendant upon the factory system sprang in large measure, it was believed, from women's employment. By leaving their homes they had not only lost the domestic virtues that were inherently theirs, but they had also undermined the position of male workers within factories. Francis Place presented the whole package deal in the *Poor Man's*

Guardian in 1835.

> If then the men refused to work in mills and factories with girls, as other trades have done, in workshops and for those masters who employ women and girls, the young women who will otherwise be degraded by factory labour will become all that can be desired as companiable wives and the whole condition of factory workers will soon be improved, the men will obtain competent wages for their maintenance.[34]

It is little wonder that modern 'feminist' historians are cynical about the attitudes of both employers and male workers and ready to argue that men's insistence on female inferiority received its just reward when cheap labour threatened their own position. Nor is it surprising that women were slow to make effective contributions to industrial and political questions when they were repeatedly being urged to fulfil their destiny as wives and mothers. One description of woman's role suggested that 'In the privacy of the domestic circle she reigns as the queen of the home, where, surrounded with the objects of her love and affection, she bestows on them her unwearied attention and unceasing care.'[35] And this idealisation occurred within the context of a movement, Chartism, which made repeated pleas for women's full participation.

Within the pre-industrial economy their participation was almost complete, and certainly much more comprehensive than it had become by the third quarter of the nineteenth century. Inside that economy, argues Sheila Lewenhak, the term 'journeyman' frequently covered both sexes, and there was widespread participation by women in eighteenth-century trade union activity.[36] The search for early women trade unionists has already produced a few examples and will doubtless in time produce a few more. In pre-Industrial Revolution Manchester, for example, as early as 1747 there was evidently a mixed society of small ware weavers in being, and in 1788 an informal union of female spinners of wool existed in Leicester, known as the Sisterhood, which stirred males to riot over the issue of pauper labour and new machinery.[37]

Short-lived, *ad hoc* groupings of women in particular trades remained a feature of the east Midlands, particularly in the lace trade, in the early decades of the nineteenth century. In 1811 the female lace-runners of Loughborough achieved immediate notoriety and enduring fame when they exhibited 'a spirit of combination' in campaigning to force a rise. By organising meetings and despatching emissaries to raise funds in neighbouring towns, all of which had their own problems in this year, they provoked the local magistrate, Parson Hardy, into issuing a warning about the illegality of their actions.[38] Nearly thirty years later their sisters in nearby Nottingham achieved what has been regarded as one of the most heroic failures of nineteenth-century female industrial protest when they organised and went on strike in 1840 in an effort to cut out the 'middlewoman' in their trade's operation. Although the women were frustrated by the depressed times in which they struck and the susceptibility of their younger members to intimidation by their mistresses, their efforts were praised for 'tact and perseverance not expected from the female character', a somewhat back-handed compliment.[39]

The Lancashire cotton industry was the setting for a large pro-portion of women's trade union activity, as it was the setting for so much else, and in the early days women appear to have had an accepted part. A powerful mixed society of spinners existed in the 1790s which had rules that specifically attributed to women equal rights over apprenticeship, and there was also a Society of Small Ware Weavers and Cotton Weavers' Union which included women.[40] On the basis of this kind of membership, women probably played an active part in the great strikes of the early nineteenth century. During the handloom weavers' strike of 1808 they were singled out by *The Times* for being more mischievous and turbulent than the men and seeming to suppose that their sex would bring them immunity from the consequences of insolent behaviour towards soldiers and special constables.[41] One, Elizabeth Walmsley, was indeed prosecuted for misdemeanour. In view of the large number of women to be found amongst the handloom weavers, an estimated half of the total being women and children by 1808, it is difficult to see how the strike could have been so effectively applied without their support.[42] In 1818, women drew equal strike pay during the Lancashire cotton spinners' strike and organised their own protests, though they were subsequently excluded from the union.[43] During the power-loom weavers' strike later in the same year, women were active in processions and gave support to the strike before the introduction of blackleg labour, and the desire of women strikers to return to work led to the notorious 'pumping' incident at Stockport when 'blackleg' workers were given a breathless soaking and some women were bound over for receiving strike pay.[44] In 1824 the women of Stockport showed greater solidarity when twelve female workers chose to share the fate of eleven males and accept a prison sentence in preference to returning to work at greatly reduced rates.[45] The subsequent hostility of male spinners, handloom weavers and particularly the skilled groups such as beamers, twisters and drawers, and their determination to exclude women from their own organisations, helped to preclude extensive female trade union activity in the cotton industry until such a time as women became firmly established in power-loom weaving, a development that encouraged more participation and militancy in the 1840s.[46]

The greatest single upsurge in women's trade unionism is undoubtedly that associated with the general unionism, and particularly the Grand National Consolidated Trades Union of 1833 – 4, when groups of unskilled workers, including women's groups, began to organise lodges and unions in trades that had never previously known them. Like so many aspects of this exciting episode, women's involvement is far from clear, and the period threw up exotic organisations like the Grand United Lodge of Operative Ladies' Maids, and all-embracing names such as the Female Grand Lodge of Miscellaneous Operatives, as well as the more self-explanatory Lodge of Female Tailors and female unions organising great varieties of working women, as those at Nottingham and Leicester.[47] The appeal of the Grand National to women was quite explicit:

> As a very large number of females among the industrious classes are exposed to great hardships and oppressions in the disposal of their labour . . . and as our Union would be manifestly incomplete without their good will and co-operation . . . we should offer them every encouragement and assistance to form themselves into lodges for the protection of their industry in every city or town where it is practicable.[48]

Women were thus expressly bidden to join the federation, and many, though an unknown number, now had their first experience of trade unionism. It has been noted that these did not include the textile workers of industrial Lancashire. Rather, it is suggested, were they the unskilled women of London, Birmingham and other towns who were engaged in the dangerous and low-paid metal trades of the west Midlands, or the low-paid sweated trades such as tailoring or bonnet-making. In Birmingham in particular women found their own cheaper labour being substituted for the higher-priced work of males; they were given direct and immediate experience of how their sex was being exploited and began to face up to the general issue of women's labour within industrial society.[49] The *Pioneer* contained letters from women who began to talk of 'the rights of labour' and 'the oppressor, our employers', and who urged women to turn to trade unionism and not to regard domestic affairs as their sole concern.[50] In trades where they were manifestly being treated unequally with men, they should command recognition for their 'natural equality' and eventually, they hoped, men would also see that their own self-interest required that women should not be paid lower rates and be in a position to undercut male workers.

It was an exhilarating period during which P.A.S. addressed herself to the Bonnet Makers of London, Hertford and Bedford and went on to establish a union of these women to raise their wages and in other ways protect their labour.[51] Not all women unionists were so aggressively self-conscious, as women. In an admittedly ambiguous situation at Derby, where some women expressed hostility to striking, almost 500 women were locked out of work through refusing to sign a declaration against contribution to union funds, and women were active in leading demonstrations in the town as well as in sending contributions from other towns, such as Birmingham.[52] In Leicester in October 1833 four dismissed workers from a worsted spinning mill, turned off because they belonged to the union, had the support of males, who reached agreement with their employers over wages but demanded the reinstatement of the women as a precondition to their return. Unfortunately for the success of the women, some men were ready to argue that 'The business of the men was entirely separate from that of the women', and the women lost their challenge.[53] Although the Grand National collapse was accompanied by the demise of most of these women's organisations that had come into temporary life as part of the general upsurge of activity, and despite the fact that the women of industrial Lancashire played little part in the movement of 1833 – 4, this was a significant period in the history of women's trade unionism for the range of women who became, albeit temporarily, involved, the nature of their arguments as they debated the role of women in the work-force, their willingness to accept the need for trade union organisation for the protection of their rights as workers, and the realisation that women would need to accept segregated organisations.

These were years of female activity within the Scottish cotton and Yorkshire woollen industries. In 1833 Glasgow women spinners and power-loom weavers combined in an effort to achieve parity with male workers on piece rates, and in March of that year a delegate meeting of no fewer than 1,000 women was said to have been held in the Lyceum Rooms to form an association 'for their mutual protection against the encroachments of tyrannical over-seers and the reductions of masters'. They elected a 'Chairwoman' and other officials to act on behalf of 12,498 female power-loom operators and proposed to raise subscriptions to cover sickness and unemployment payments for members.[54] The following February the *Aberdeen Herald* reported a 'turn-out' of 140 female reelers and spinners at Broadford to counteract a threatened reduction of 6*d*. Accompanied by a blind fiddler, they paraded the streets with a flag, before attending a meeting at which they resolved that their proceedings were legitimate, that the standard of liberty was now unfurled, that they would no longer submit to oppression and low wages, and that their sisters from Poyernook to Grandholme should co-operate with them. After collecting 15*s* 8*d* from bystanders, they retired peacefully to their homes.[55] Some support was also received by the Scottish female spool of 'pirn' winders who worked for male weavers. They organised unions in Hamilton, Airdrie and Irvine, and sought a rise in piece rates in October 1836. They were given backing by the *Weavers' Journal*, which exhorted male workers to give more support to their cause.[56]

The West Riding also had its problems. On 1 February 1832, about 500 workpeople, chiefly young women and boys, in the power-loom stuff manufacture at Burley Mill, near Leeds, went on strike to resist a cut in wages. They were probably unsuccessful, because some were reported to have returned to work and others to have left their jobs.[57] One of the most publicised incidents within the subsidiary branches of the wool trade occurred at Peep Green, Hartshead, in May 1833, when a crowd said to constitute 1,500 women resolved not to set any more cards, required in the combing process, for less than a halfpenny per thousand and at the same time condemned truck payments which were still prevalent amongst employers. The *Leeds Mercury* found this display of female independence more fraught with menace to established institutions than the education of 'the lower orders', a nice judgement, which it is still too soon to confirm or reject.[58] In the same month women were charged at Wakefield with having assaulted a 'black sheep'.[59]

Other grievances were expressed by the female power-loom weavers in Brand's woollen mill, Bradford, in 1838, who complained of warped looms and an inability to make a living on these machines at existing rates. After being fined for leaving work unfinished, the women were forced to return, save one who opted for a month in the House of Correction.[60] Greater success was enjoyed in that same year by striking female cloth weavers at Elland, who successfully attacked a cart containing cloth woven by blackleg labour and compelled its return to Balmforth's mill. The owner, 'being determined not to be beaten by women', attempted to deliver the load himself, but he was forced back by an angry crowd of 200 women and eventually agreed to take back his weavers at the old prices for which the women had been on strike.[61] A similar resolution was shown in November 1838 by women workers in Cookson's Plate Glass Factory in Newcastle, where the owner had tried unilaterally to change the methods of paying his workers and had to be coerced into abandoning his plans by successive strikes, having boasted that he would sooner leave the factory than 'concede one iota to the women'.[62]

The increased militancy and female self-consciousness of the 1830s could hardly have left the women of the Lancashire cotton industry untouched, despite their absence from the Grand National. During the early 1830s there had been greater reluctance among the female cotton workers to face up to the general predicament of workers in industry than there had been in, for instance, the Birmingham area. Perhaps this occurred in part because the women in the cotton industry were less obviously discriminated against on sex grounds than their counterparts elsewhere. Whatever the cause of their backwardness, it was eroded somewhat in the prevailing atmosphere of the late 1830s, when the anti-Poor Law movement and Chartism both encouraged women to think more about their position. More important, women's own position within the factory population was becoming more secure and more dominant. By 1835 females were as numerous as males within the cotton factories of Cheshire and Lancashire combined, and they were no longer nervously occupying merely the peripheral, unskilled positions but were, with the rapid growth of power weaving after 1825, controlling a central process within the industry and becoming a more numerous body than the male spinners who had for so long dominated the trade.[63] By the early

1840s women's labour was in short supply in south Lancashire, and women could enjoy parity of status with men as the first attempts were made in these years to organise power-loom weavers, piecers and card-room hands. Rebuffed by the men after the 1818 strike and excluded from the men's unions, the women remained fairly quiescent during their early years as power-loom weavers in the factories, from 1825, apparently not wishing to risk their new position by conflict with their employers. By the 1840s the situation had changed somewhat, and women again came to the fore as industrial conflict shifted noticeably from the spinning to the weaving sector of the trade.[64]

In March 1840 there occurred in Stockport a strike of women throstle spinners and in the April a strike of some 4,000 power-loom weavers, following a mass meeting said to have been attended by 2,500 of whom 1,832 were women. The strike motion was seconded by a Mrs Wrigley, who invited all women workers to show good sense and stand solidly with the men in this dispute.

> In 1829, she stood by the turnouts, living upon nettles and coarse food; but God forbid that any creature should slave as she had done, for thirty-two years, and be bated all the while; and now the tyrants wanted to take away the last pittances. (Cries of 'Hear, hear') The women were the majority of the weavers, and if they would stick true to their cause, they would succeed. Women! will you stand by the rights of the men for your own benefit. ('We will') Men! will you stand by and protect the women? ('Like glue'; laughter.)

This exercise in solidarity between the sexes was strengthened by the assurance of Thomas Leonard that men did not want to replace women in power-loom weaving, and women certainly appear to have exercised major control over picketing and other strike measures. Many women were arrested. Jane Lowry, Mary Ann Ridgway and Maria Ancoats were charged with conspiracy to force certain weavers to leave their employment and organising pickets; another group of nine were charged with intimidating Margaret Tinsley by picketing, groaning and shouting uncomplimentary expressions including 'knobstick', 'Baa lamb' and 'black sheep'. All defendants were convicted and sent to prison.[65] They had shown a remarkable degree of militancy and readiness to co-operate with male weavers.

Women were very active in the events constituting the Plug Plot riots of 1842, as will be seen, and in 1843 were much involved in strikes, especially around Ashton. In May sixteen mills, having a work-force two-thirds of whom were women, were closed by strikes, and women, not surprisingly, attended meetings and demonstrations in large numbers eventually resolving to form a union of the weavers of Ashton. In Wigan a strike of 300 women and children and 100 or more men lasted for four months, and women were prominent in strike leadership at Stalybridge, where three women made up half the deputation that negotiated with the masters.[65] This new confidence and new role encouraged a changed attitude to the Ten Hour Movement as it reformed in the middle of the decade.

As workers who sometimes found themselves organised in trade unions, women inevitably became involved also to some degree in the political issues and popular campaigns arising out of industrial employment or trade union organisation. One such issue was that of the Dorchester labourers, or Tolpuddle Martyrs, of 1834. It had been a woman who gave the alarm when the men were arrested, and working women made their contributions to a union fund established to support the wives and families of the transported men.[67] They also took part in the demonstrations that were held throughout the country against the sentence passed on the men. In Nottingham, for instance, on 31 March, a crowd of 2,000 trade unionists assembled on the Forest to make their protest, and towards the end of the meeting the Nottingham Female Union appeared. Both unions then marched in procession back to the Market Square, accompanied by a band which played the national anthem and 'Praise God from whom all blessings flow', which seems as inappropriate now as it must have seemed to the more discerning participants at the time.[68]

A bigger and more complex movement was that for factory reform, which incorporated the campaign against children's employment and the demand for the ten-hour day for adults. This movement brings out so many of the ambiguities in the position of working women, who were by no means unanimously enthusiastic about the attempts of others to give them a shorter day. In the woollen mill districts of Yorkshire, women, though not members of any of the short-time committees that helped organise the campaign under Oastler's leadership, none the less made an important contribution to the emotional atmosphere in which the agitation was conducted. In the words of Samuel Kydd:

> The Yorkshire meetings had features peculiarly their own. The tears, the smiles, the songs, the vows of the women and children, the sense of indignation which now and again shot from the eyes of all when the nobler feelings of their hearts were appealed to, will, by those who witnessed these scenes, never be forgotten . . . then and there, a mother clasping an infant to her breast, kissing it and exclaiming: 'Factory slave thou shall never be', gave to the proceedings a dramatic interest, remarkable, intense, and exciting.[69]

Women faithfully attended the meetings and demonstrations addressed by and on behalf of Oastler or Sadler in Yorkshire, but in Lancashire they were missing. There the movement appears to have been firmly in the hands of Doherty and the male spinners and to have concentrated on the question of technological innovation in the cotton mills, with women appearing to have played virtually no part. Yorkshire audiences might be told by John Fielden that shorter hours would be beneficial to women, but his promises to return woman to 'her proper social rank' and make her again 'the centre of a system of social delights' sounded very like removing her entirely from factory employment. This was occasionally made explicit by indiscreet male references to the way in which new machines had resulted in the employment of women and children to the exclusion of those who ought to labour, namely the men. Even the implicit message was sufficient for the perceptive women of Lancashire, who, in expressing indifference or outright hostility, as they did to the Factory Commissioners, defended, as they believed, their very living, believing that regulation could lead to reduced pay and possibly total exclusion from the factories.[70] This was not a pleasant prospect to the 'Female Operatives of Todmorden', who saw servitude and dressmaking as the only other available options.[71] At a time when women were establishing a precarious foothold as power-loom weavers in the factories, they seem to have eschewed involvement in causes of this kind, seeking to avoid direct confrontation with their employers, having neither the wage levels nor the security of tenure to feel safe from the reprisals that active involvement might have precipitated.

In the agitation that preceded the passage of the Ten Hour Act in 1847 and that which accompanied attempts to enforce it, male spinners still retained their leadership in the movement and still sought increased employment opportunities for men. The argument that shorter hours would give women more time at home still looked like the proposition that women's place was in the home. Not surprisingly, many female factory workers showed a lack of interest in this cause and 'Elizabeth' of Todmorden wrote to complain of 'the apathy that is manifested by my sex generally'; shorter hours still carried the implication of smaller pay packets. 'Elizabeth' deplored this holding off, maintaining that women's mainstream participation in the industry demanded their mainstream participation in its reform and its politics and that women should be agitating as workers rather than seeing themselves as a sectional interest.[72] This was now easier to contemplate, for women were less vulnerable in their employment, their labour was in demand, their role a central one, and their wages steady. The time had come to question the need for long hours of toil in poor conditions and to consider the possibility that they could now afford to be working shorter hours. Although women were not particularly active in the events leading up to the 1847 Act, they seem to have taken a prominent part in agitations to ensure that men as well as women enjoyed the benefit of the new Act, being particularly forward in the strikes and meetings of 1848 – 9 to frustrate the relay and shift systems by which the masters sought to undermine the new legislation.[73] Yet, for all this new-found willingness of female factory operatives to see themselves as workers and be involved in workers', rather than women's, causes, the ambiguity over the woman's place remained, for some women saw shorter hours as a step towards complete withdrawal from factory employment and single women were ready at times to urge this upon their married sisters as the proper course of conduct. Conflicting ideals of a reformed factory system and an existence totally outside it continued to complicate the lives of many women in industry. Nor was the choice a simple one for those other women who apparently went to considerable lengths to defy government legislation that prevented them in 1844 from working underground.[74]

The demonstrations and riots that frequently preceded or accompanied strikes were other occasions for women's involvement in industrial protest. After the south Wales coal and iron strikes of 1816, two women were sent for trial for their part in the disturbances, for women had joined the crowds of striking men in both the Merthyr and Newport areas.[75] More impressive was the contribution of women to the demonstrations of stocking-knitters in Nottingham in August 1819, a time of deepest depression in the hosiery trade, when the men resorted to daily processions through the town to draw attention to their plight. On the 19th the men were led by a great number of women, and afterwards groups of men, accompanied by their wives and children, carried boards through the streets bearing the messages 'Pity our distresses,' 'We ask for bread,' and 'Pity our children.'[76] This passive conduct was superseded in April 1837 by a much more violent response when employers declined to give out work or offered it only at abated prices. This time 'The workmen's wives and children congregated in the streets in great numbers and levied contributions upon the provision shops to a considerable extent.' The police had great difficulty in restoring peace in a situation where an industrial grievance had resurrected a form of protest closely akin to the old food riot.[77]

The fullest participation of women in industrial protest occurred during the so-called Plug Plot riots of August 1842, when their role was an extremely varied one, though many of their activities were peripheral rather than central to the main issues of wages and trade stoppages. In these they played a limited part. The crowd of 1,000 or more which visited Stalybridge Mill and brought it to a halt in early August was said to have been about one-third female in composition as men and women, mixed indiscriminately, followed the 'big lads' in their mission of persuasion.[78] In Rochdale a mob, said to number 10,000, led by women eight or ten abreast and 'singing some lively song', stopped the mills of the town. Afterwards 'about fifty women went in Tweedale's Hotel and were treated with a good dinner and plenty to drink, for which they were extremely grateful, being', it was said, 'at a distance from home'.[79] Some days later the Rochdale crowd led the turn-outs in surrounding towns and villages, including in their ranks girls believed to be not more than twelve or fourteen years of age and wearing heavy clogs, who walked over twenty miles without the least refreshment, a distressing sight as they returned 'haggard, tired, and lame'.[80] Girls of unspecified age were also active in Bolton, marching to Temple Mill and causing it to be stopped, and in Manchester too 'a number of females assembled in the neighbourhood of Great Ancoats street, and proceed [sic] through the main streets, their numbers all the while augmenting. Their object was to stop the various mills not already stopped.' After some success at one mill they encountered resistance at another, whereupon 'they poured a tremendous volley of stones into the windows, burst open the outer door, and were about to rush into the factory, when a posse of police arrived.'[81]

Such direct participation in the strikes, the closing of mills at the instigation of crowds, in which women played a prominent and noted part, is virtually the limit of female involvement in the industrial action itself. Women appear to have played no part in the deliberations of the trades of Manchester and district, and their absence is highlighted by a meeting on 15 August of spinners, power-loom weavers, self-acting mule workers and card-room hands. No women were present, for placards announcing the meeting had warned them to 'remain at home until the decision of the meeting was known'.[82] At general meetings of the trade, representatives of the workers were men, even where women were presumably heavily involved, as in power-loom weaving. A week later, on 22 August, a further meeting of the trades was held in Manchester which was attended by 150 men and no women.[83]

Women's role was essentially in the crowd scenes, sometimes as principals and sometimes merely as extras. Where meetings or demonstrations were held in August 1842, women were usually present in large numbers, whether in Yorkshire towns like Barnsley, Leeds or Huddersfield, or in the cotton towns surrounding Manchester. At Leeds the women hissed and hooted at the soldiers and police and subjected them to the same treatment in suburban Holbeck. Despite this only one woman was arrested in Leeds; she was Hannah Scorah, aged 39, of Hunslet, but she was not on the list of 27 people committed for trial in York for their part in the Yorkshire disturbances.[84] In Manchester a large number of women turned up for a 6.30 a.m. meeting on 11 August, after a previous day of violence in the town, and this day brought attacks upon shops where women were active in demanding bread or money from the owners.[85] In Leicestershire, crowds of youths and women gathered round the Plough Inn at Loughborough to taunt the pensioners and the special constables who were based there, whilst demonstrations in the county town brought out large numbers of women, including some with small children in their arms.[86] At the so-called 'Battle of Mapperley Hills' in Nottingham, one woman was allegedly brought into premature labour through the brutality of the soldiers who dispersed the crowd.[87]

On at least two occasions women took control of such meetings in Lancashire to hold unofficial impromptu services. On Friday, 12 August, at 5 a.m., when the county's gentry were probably bagging their first grouse of the season, a meeting in Rochdale was started with the singing of a hymn. The assembled multitude was then addressed by a woman 'in a very animated manner'. Having advised poor men to shun the ale-house and look to their wives and families, she likened them to Christ who had been 'deserted in the day of tribulation by the rich and wealthy' and who chose the poor fishermen of Galilee to preach his message. 'The state shepherds, dressed in fine linen, whose object was to fleece them' could never, she said, be considered as guardians of the fishermen's tradition. 'She went on in this strain', ran the report, 'for some time.'[88] Her performance was equalled only at Cronkeyshaw by 'a respectable-looking woman, nearly 60 years of age, dressed as a Methodist, or one of the society of friends'. This person was handed into a wagon, where she read 'the parable of the great supper' from St Luke, which she followed by an exhortation to the crowd to stand firm, 'like the Israelites of old'.[89]

Equally remarkable, and a more common phenomenon, was the capacity of women to travel long distances to spread their message of solidarity from one town to another. Leigh was visited by 2,000 men, women and children from Eccles and Patricroft.[90] Derby was visited by 1,200 colliers, accompanied by women, from surrounding areas, and the distances covered by the young women of Rochdale have already been noted.[91] The most stirring feat was that of the 'two or three hundred girls or young women' from Todmorden who marched in procession from the very borders of Lancashire into the Yorkshire mill town of Halifax, singing hymns and psalms. When the Riot Act had been read, the women, though committing no acts of violence against persons or property, 'were at this encounter the more valiant of the two' sexes; 'approaching to the very necks of the horses, they declared they would rather die than starve; and if the soldiers were determined to charge, they might kill them.'[92] Another peaceful demonstration was that of the hundreds of women, the wives and other relatives of men on strike, who went in a body to Oldham Town Hall to demand poor relief from the overseers; 'those gentlemen', it is reported, 'were too much engaged', and the women dispersed, bringing to a disappointing end an episode with a fairly promising beginning.[93]

Not all women's demonstrations were peaceful, and it would be difficult to distinguish between the sexes in terms of their relative capacity for violence. In Burslem, Staffordshire, several women were taken into custody for demolishing and stripping pawnbrokers' shops. Having demanded the return of goods that had been pledged, especially items of clothing, they found their way into shops, 'getting not their own property but anything that came to their hands, and taking many things belonging to other persons'. Nine women, 'mostly youthful, several of delicate and decent appearance', were committed, mainly for pilfering plate and other items of value from houses that had been fired.[94]

But it was the Lancashire women who were the most violent. In Wharf Street, Preston, women collected broken stones to be used for macadamising road surfaces and supplied mob leaders with 'ammunition' to be thrown at police officers and soldiers.[95] During an afternoon of the previous week a crowd consisting chiefly of women had attacked a mill at Ardwick Island, Manchester, breaking all its windows and doing damage to the value of £40. Later the same party had attacked the dye-works in Ancoats Vale belonging to Messrs Barlow and Sons.[96] On 10 August, another crowd of several hundred, including women carrying sticks, forced the gates and broke the windows of the Manchester gas works premises, and on the same day Newtown police station was attacked and gutted. Most prisoners taken after these incidents were men, but a few were women.[97] Margaret Clare allegedly 'broke one of the policeman's faces with a stone, scratched another in the face, broke a coach window, and also broke several things in the lock-up'. Her defence was that a policeman had struck her with his truncheon and she then tore his face; she was only sorry she had not possessed a good sword, for 'she would have made him smart for it'. Catherine Grimes, also remanded, was charged with being in a rioting crowd, 'cursing and swearing at the mob for running away from the police, and being violent at other times'.[98]

The prize performance was undoubtedly that of young Jane Carney, the only female arrested on the spot, a mere eleven years of age when convicted of having taken a leading part in the destruction of the Newtown police station. She was seen in an upper room of the building throwing out articles to be destroyed by the people down below and exhorting the crowds to greater fervour. The jurors at the Special Commission at Liverpool found her guilty of being riotously assembled and of feloniously destroying a police station but recommended mercy on account of her age. Men convicted on similar counts received sentences of up to fifteen years' transportation; almost all the persons tried were men and the whole of those convicted.[99]

The most remarkable thing about women's involvement in the Plug Plot riots is not their contribution to the industrial issues that prompted the turn-outs, but the diffuse nature of the protest that developed and their widely ranging activities within this protest movement. It marked a resurgence of the politics of physical confrontation, albeit in association with a movement for constitutional reform.

Any attempt at assessing the successes and achievements of women in industrial organisation and protest must avoid the temptation to claim too much. Women on occasions exercised effective leadership of crowd action, as in the Plug Plot riots of 1842, the triumph of the Elland weavers who successfully combated blackleg labour in 1838, or even the Newcastle Miners' strike of 1832, when Elizabeth Carr, a miner's wife, gave the signal to riot during a series of evictions; when carried from her own house in a chair, she seized a policeman's hat, flourished it above her head, and cheered on the exasperated mob.[100] Most of the time, though not always, women were responding to short-term economic hardship and acting spontaneously, and they left behind no permanent structures or even much in the way of philosophical discussion about the rights of women within industry or within the trade union movement. There were, of course, a few exceptions. Mary Zugg, who in 1844 organised the previously active female bookbinders employed by the London-based British and Foreign Bible Society, which paid its members an average wage of 5s 11d, is one of the first women's trade union leaders to have made a sufficient impact for her name to be recorded and remembered.[101] P.A.S., who organised the bonnet-makers of the south-east in 1834, produced probably the fullest and most carefully thought out statement of the need for women to unionise and their own responsibility for improving their lot: 'Come to the Union sisters, old and young, rich and poor . . . Children as yet unborn must have to remember that there was woman as well as men in the Union.'[102] And there were the women factory workers of the Lancashire cotton industry who, by the middle of the century, were taking steps to help safeguard the ten-hour day for the whole trade. But despite these it would be true to say that women's trade union activities suffered from all the weaknesses that beset those of the men in the first half of the nineteenth century, and more besides. There were no highly skilled groups of women to establish 'New Model Unions', and the vast majority of unskilled females suffered the same fate as the vast mass of unskilled, unorganised, non-unionised males. And besides contending with all the difficulties of the unskilled males, women had to face the commonly accepted view that they had no legitimate place in the work-force anyway, let alone in the trade union organisations created to protect that place.

5 'PETTICOAT REFORMERS'

The emergence of women as a force in British politics occurs in that post-Napoleonic War period which also produced the first popular working-class reform movements. Before this time there had been popular movements in the shape of food riots, reform movements such as that of the London Corresponding Society which involved an artisan elite, and revolutionary movements of obscure history and unknown strength which drew other working-class men into politics. But prior to 1816 there had been no open political reform movements which attracted large numbers of working-class men and became national in scope. Similarly with women's involvement, the pre-1816 years had produced little popular participation in political causes. The 'revolutionary underground' was almost certainly a male monopoly if the insurrectionary movements of post-war Britain offer any guidance to its earlier composition, and the same is probably true of the reform societies. Gwyn Williams records that at the October meeting of the London Corresponding Society at Copenhagen House in 1795 'hordes of women and children' took part in what was probably one of the largest gatherings ever to assemble in London, but he relates this to the famine conditions of this year and not to any conscious turning of women towards political processes.[1]

The riot was still their popular form of expression, even when there were political causes involved, as in the Gordon Riots of 1780 or in the anti-militia and anti-recruitment riots of the same period. These were particularly extensive in Scotland, and, though only 6 per cent of those arrested and charged in connection with them were women, it has none the less been shown that women were very actively involved in many disturbances and displayed a courage and at times a violence to equal their contributions to many food-rioting situations.[2] Even in England, as late as March 1812, when three men of Brighouse were on trial for riot and assault upon a recruiting party, it was reported that a crowd of up to a hundred had been spurred on by a woman who had cried out 'Murder them if they do not go away.'[3] Yet these riots, despite their apparent political content, were more concerned with issues that affected the domestic economy, the family and personal relations. The Scottish women had protested that it was a hard thing to bring up children alone and that they were not prepared to let their menfolk be carried off; their attacks upon press gangs and military escorts and the crowds dramatically raised, as at East Tranent in 1797 by a woman beating a drum (she was subsequently killed in clashes with the troops), were all a reflection of immediate economic and domestic concerns and not some pronunciation on great national issues.[4]

When the war ended and 'whilst', in Samuel Bamford's memorable words, 'the laurels were yet cool on the brows of our victorious soldiers on their second occupation of Paris, the elements of convulsion were at work amongst the masses of our labouring population'. Bamford listed the riots and demonstrations throughout England and Scotland against high prices, shortages, the corn laws and machinery, arising generally out of economic distress, and recorded how William Cobbett succeeded in diverting all the discontented groups from direct forms of action by persuading them that their troubles had one common cause — 'misgovernment', and one 'common corrective' — parliamentary reform.[5] The accuracy of the Cobbett diagnosis, and indeed the Cobbett prescription of a remedy, are more open to question than Bamford supposed, but he was at least right to recognise that parliamentary reform became the grand panacea for working-class discontent and that direct action would never recover its former hold. Perhaps women made the transition less swiftly and less easily, but by the middle of 1819 independent female radical reform societies were in existence and women too were coming to accept the supposed veracity of what William Cobbett was telling them.

Lancashire was the home of these early societies as it was the centre of so much else during this period, and it could be argued that any attempt to explain Lancashire's primacy in this additional area would be a mere stating of the obvious. As the area which first experienced industrialisation and urbanisation in their modern form, which forcibly resisted technological change in the 1770s, which campaigned for a minimum wage in the early years of the nineteenth century, and which was already organising petitions for parliamentary reform in 1812, Lancashire was the usual pace setter. Its women had broken the new spinning machinery in the eighteenth century and been organised in the cotton trade unions in the 1790s. They had been hanged for food rioting in 1812 and charged along with male Luddites in that year for participating in attacks upon mills. There is nothing surprising about their readiness to join the post-war parliamentary reform movement, which must surely have occurred irrespective of the patronage of Samuel Bamford, who took personal credit for their initiation into the formal procedures of male reformers, though not for first inviting their attendance at meetings. Writing of a meeting in Saddleworth he recorded in much-quoted sentences:

> I, in the course of an address, insisted on the right, and the propriety also, of females who were present at such assemblages, voting by show of hands, for, or against the resolution. This was a new idea; and the women who attended numerously on that bleak ridge were mightily pleased with it — and the men being nothing dissentient when the resolution was put, the women held up their hands, amid much laughter; and ever from that time women voted at radical meetings.[6]

Bamford's personal intervention may or may not have been significant, but it is significant that this first voting endeavour was greeted with laughter, for the appearance of women in politics, this sudden leap forward in consciousness, was not something to which men, even male reformers, adjusted easily.[7]

Woolers' *Black Dwarf* illustrated this proposition well. Satire was its chosen weapon and no subject lent itself more readily to satirical treatment than women in politics. In February 1817, *The Black Dwarf* had been much annoyed to learn of a reform meeting at Newcastle-under-Lyme at which prostitutes, 'hardened as ministers of state', had been scattered amongst the audience to create opposition, 'a body of those creatures who disgrace the female sex by their want of its chief ornament, and outdo ours in every species of wickedness and brutality'.[8] Fortunately, the memory of their deeds was to be effaced the following year by the action of Mary Ann Tocker who, indicted for a libel against a Mr Gurney who, she had alleged, was unfit to administer the laws of the country, chose to defend herself. Not only that, she disregarded and virtually humiliated the judge, securing her acquittal and successfully arguing that 'truth is not a libel.' Perverted law had been vanquished and 'the barbarous offspring of the Star Chamber, now so effectually disgraced and overcome by a Woman', ought never to be heard again 'exerting its pestilential influence against the Rights of Man'. However pleasing the verdict, the inherent dangers in the woman's success were that 'the tongues of the whole sex, with their well known and pleasing velocity, will be let loose.'[9] Ms Tocker was acclaimed, but the precedent was alarming. *The Black Dwarf*, in fact, was as much responsible for encouraging debate as for reporting it and helped to publicise the cause of women in politics by affecting great concern:

> Their arguments are very forcible. They say that since the men abandoned the cause of freedom, they will support it. They say freedom was a woman, and therefore every woman ought to be free. Man, they add, has shamefully deserted his post:— and has no right to control woman:— since he has lost the power of defending himself:— that the grovelling slaves of Oliver and Castles are not proper masters for freeborn woman — that woman can expect no protection from the cowards that cannot protect themselves![10]

It fitted the style of the *Dwarf* to argue that an administration of young women was to be preferred to the present administration of old ones, but the women who were supposedly being quoted are not identified and a certain licence seems to have been enjoyed by the writer in attributing his own words to others.[11] It was a good tactic to argue that 'man has confessed himself a slave' as a means of stimulating some male response, but reactions were probably not entirely as planned.[12] One woman denied any wish for powers of oratory or the right to vote, seeking to know how a mother might best fulfil her duty to educate her children in correct notions of civil and religious liberty and human rights in general; another rejoiced in the breach made in 'the exclusive privileges of the gentlemen of the long robe'; whilst a third, Caroline of Pimlico, produced the most stirring response, that 'we are not merely to be valued for our talents in the nursery, or our graces in the ballroom . . . some of us, at least, are destined to soar as high in the regions of fame, as the most distinguished patriots among them.'[13] Little wonder that the males retaliated with reference to women's unbeatable weapons, 'eye spears', 'tongue spears' and 'magical grape shot, composed entirely of hair'.[14] Others challenged in verse:

> O say, lovely pleader, while thus you require,
> For your sex a political station,
> What more can a lady's ambition desire,
> Than to lord o'er us lords of creation?[15]

An appeal to the stereotype was the resort of the frightened male, who continued, more mischievously, to ask:

> Can a soul-beaming glance be resisted by steel?
> What is reason to woman's opinion?[16]

If this appeal failed, there were others to add to its persuasive powers:

> Sweet revolutionary termagants,
> Dear sisters, mothers, daughters, nieces, aunts,
> Wives, spinsters, widows, prudes, and jilts,
> Quit, for a moment quit your stilts,
> Give up these whirligig tetotum fancies.[17]

The argument was very urbane and witty, at least on the male side, and doubtless *The Black Dwarf* was amused by the spectre that he had helped to raise. It was a spectre, because the women's political reform societies that were to appear in the following year were not the work of women aspiring to soar high in the regions of fame, but ordinary people from ordinary backgrounds with modest ambitions arising from very real, down-to-earth grievances.

In late June 1819 a meeting took place in Blackburn which the *Annual Register* was to describe as 'An entirely novel and truly portentous circumstance'.[18] It established the Blackburn Female Reform Society, the object of which was 'to assist the male population of this country to obtain their rights and liberties'; under its rules each member was required to contribute one penny per week towards the expenses, not of their own organisation but of the male union societies of Blackburn; in addition, members 'individually and collectively pledge themselves to use their utmost endeavours to instil into the minds of their children a deep and rooted hatred to their tyrannical rulers'.[19] On 5 July the members of this new organisation were formally presented to a general meeting of Blackburn reformers, which produced a 'most interesting and enchanting scene'. The committee members of the Female Society

> were very neatly dressed for the occasion, and each wore a green favour in her bonnet and cap . . . The ladies ascended the hustings amidst the reiterated acclamations of the people . . . one

of them with becoming diffidence and respect . . . presented him
with a most beautiful Cap of Liberty, made of scarlet silk or
satin, lined with green, with a serpentined gold lace, terminating
with a rich gold tassel . . . the tear of welcome sympathy seemed
to trickle from every eye — 'God bless the women' was uttered
from every tongue. Could the cannibal Castlereagh have witnessed this noble expression of public sentiment, he must have
had a heart of brass, if it had not struck him dead to the ground.'
In a 'short emphatic speech' their leader Mrs. Alice Kitchen
asked the Chairman 'Will you, sir, accept this token of our
respect to those brave men who are nobly struggling for liberty
and life; by placing it at the head of your banner, you will confer
a lasting obligation on the Female Reformers of Blackburn.[20]

Very soon the women of Blackburn were not alone. On 8 July a
notice appeared advertising a foundation meeting for the
Manchester Female Reform Society the following week to enlist
subscribers and to adopt resolutions.[21] Within a week it was
reported that 1,000 members had already enrolled.[22] At the same
time the Female Union Society of Stockport was busy formulating
its rules and issuing declarations of their intention to help the male
reformers, to instil proper principles into the minds of their
children, and in general to emulate the women of Sparta by never
deserting the standard of liberty.[23] Their 36 founder members had
grown to 84 by the third meeting and they were reported as having
followed the Methodist practice of dividing up into classes of
twelve members, each group having a leader who collected the
penny per week subscription.[24] These Lancashire associations were
quickly cited as an inspiration and an example to the women of
other towns in Yorkshire, Nottinghamshire and beyond.[25] At a
reform meeting in Nottingham in mid-July the speakers urged the
local women to respond to the call and the cause, and new societies
were reported at this time in Paisley, Leeds, Yeadon and 'a variety
of other places'.[26] The other places were shortly to include Royton
and Ashton in Lancashire and Halifax and Hull in Yorkshire.[27] In
addition, there was a West of England Female Union Society which
forwarded its rules to the editor of the *Manchester Observer*,
through Elizabeth Russell, its 'Chairwoman', to show that 'the
aims of liberty from the North' had reached the West, and it has
been suggested that some attempt might have been made to draw
the various societies together into some kind of federation.[28] What-

ever the truth of that, it seems probable that a dozen or so purely female societies came into existence in the weeks before Peterloo and that together they added a new dimension to both working-class politics and women's public life.

Their activities were many and varied. The mainstay was the weekly meeting with its opportunities for the making of speeches and the passing of resolutions, themselves fairly novel activities for women's involvement. Subscriptions had to be collected, the cele-brated 'Cap of Liberty' to be made and subsequently presented, banners prepared, and rallies and demonstrations planned. At the public meetings women attended in great numbers, for the first time in a situation of equality with men, proclaiming their identity with their banners, and showing their solidarity with male reformers in such a way as to encourage the view 'we are one' as a comment on this new co-operation.[29] In their praise for and presentations to Henry Hunt and William Cobbett, the female societies showed a fervour and degree of hero worship that have sometimes been regarded as excessive, but both these popular leaders appeared glad to strengthen the basis of their mass following by the addition of innumerable female supporters. Any suggestion that the women indulged in much rhetoric and achieved little in the way of positive action is a charge that can equally well be applied to their male counterparts of this period.

The most important question raised by this new phenomenon in British politics is that of what prompted women to turn towards politics and seek this new form of expression for their grievances and discontents. Part of the explanation is doubtless to be found in terms of the increased experience of women in industrial Lancashire as wage earners outside as well as inside the home and their adoption of radical politics, along with the men, in conditions of post-war depression. We have shared your misery, ran one argument; now we wish to share your political endeavour in an effort to do something about it.[30] The connection between economic grievance and political remedies, a link which food rioters usually stopped short of making, was now for the first time being quite explicitly stated, though not necessarily in terms that indicate any clear consciousness of a class role within the industrial system;

> the best artizan, manufacturers, and labourers of this vast com-munity [had been reduced] to a state of wretchedness and misery

. . . to the very verge of beggary and ruin . . . our houses which once bore ample testimony of our industry and cleanliness . . . now robbed of all their ornaments, and our beds, that once afforded us cleanliness, health, and sweet repose, are now torn away from us.

The alleged perpetrators of these outrages, catalogued by the Blackburn women, were not the mill-owners or other masters but 'the present borough-mongering and Jesuitical system' and the 'unfeeling tax gatherer, to satisfy the greatest monsters of cruelty, the borough-mongering tyrants'.[31] Similarly with the Female Reformers of Manchester, the 'poverty, wretchedness, tyranny, and injustice', 'the tattered garments to cover the nakedness of our forlorn and destitute families' were all attributed to 'the lazy Borough-mongering Eagle of destruction' that had 'nearly picked bare the bones of those who labour'; taxation was again condemned as having 'nearly annihilated our once flourishing trade and commerce', 'driving our merchants and manufacturers to poverty and degradation'.[32] When Susannah Saxton framed this address she quite evidently viewed the manufacturers as sufferers in a common cause rather than the enemy against whom working people needed to agitate: the enemy were clearly the borough-mongers of the unreformed Parliament and the taxes which they perpetrated. If, as has been claimed, the female reformers made an explicit connection between the cause of parliamentary reform and economic circumstances prevailing in post-war Lancashire, they did so in the apparent belief that political reform in itself would bring cures to their social and economic ills;[33] their complaints against the unreformed Parliament differed little from those of the manufacturers who employed them and their husbands. The borough-mongering aristocrats were doubtless somewhat indifferent to the fate of the poor but fairly remote, it would be assumed, from the lives of the women who joined the reform societies. Cobbett, applauded by Bamford for his success in persuading so many diverse groups that their answers lay in the reform of Parliament, had indeed achieved remarkable success in converting the women of Lancashire to his political approach. He even persuaded some of them to stop buying heavily taxed commodities, tea and coffee, and replace them with his own recommended herbal blends.[34]

They did not, of course, find it easy to fit readily into political activities. The whole situation was too novel. When Mr Fitton addressed the Stockport Union for the promotion of human happiness in July 1819, he confessed that it was unusual for him to have to address an assembly of reformers as 'Ladies and Gentlemen', and the women themselves were constantly aware of this problem and inhibited by it.[35] At the second meeting of the Stockport Female Reform Society on 19 July, at which there were men present, at least during the early stages of the meeting, Mrs Hallworth, on being elected President, requested the gentlemen to withdraw

> with a view that if in our debates (for it is something new for women to turn political orators) we should for want of knowledge make any blunders we should be laughed at, to prevent which we should prefer being by ourselves . . . the male brethren immediately obliged.

In view of continuing problems concerning the appropriate form of address to women in the chair, it is hardly surprising that on this occasion speakers struggled with 'Mrs. President and ladies' and 'Mrs. President and sisters'.[36] These difficulties help to explain why the Blackburn Society, for instance, found it necessary to apologise for any feminine weaknesses or impotency which they might be displaying, and for what they themselves described as 'interference' in the country's politics.[37] Even as late as May 1820, the female reformers of Manchester, when making proposals for the relief of imprisoned radicals, still felt obliged to note the different opinions that existed on the propriety of women engaging in politics.[38]

Such defensive attitudes, which are perfectly understandable, nevertheless made the women very vulnerable to hostile comment passed by those who were not happy to encourage these first steps towards political involvement. A particularly antagonistic reception was that given by the *Manchester Chronicle*, which labelled the Blackburn Female Reformers as 'women well known to be of the most abandoned of their sex' and described their presentation at the Blackburn reform meeting as a 'most disgusting scene'. The same edition of the paper attacked an unnamed 'Reforming Female' for visiting Leigh and disseminating revolutionary principles there, including instructions on how to manufacture pikes.[39] No one else had quite such damning charges to lay against the women as this one, and it is rather difficult to accept the veracity of this accusation. More legitimate, though equally hostile, was the paper's questioning of whether women would not be better employed in activities other than politics; the view was that alternative employment was to be preferred to their current proceedings, which presented 'a spectacle very revolting to those actions of female delicacy which are so natural to Englishmen'.[40] It was even held against the women who attended an allegedly seditious meeting at Leigh that 'their dress and appearance bore no marks of that misery and want which were said to prevail in Leigh and the neighbourhood'.[41] Reformers with dirty faces and tattered garments would evidently have been more acceptable, though these would doubtless have prompted the accusation that women were neglecting their homes and families by their political activity, an argument which they were always most anxious to counter. There was little to be done about the condemnation which they received from members of their own sex among the upper classes or the semi-official reprimand from a government-financed journal which expressed the hope that Parliament would 'make it a felony without benefit of clergy, for women to bear any active or ostensible part' in what were described as 'seditious meetings'.[42]

Against such antagonism the female reformers had to take what comfort they could from the backing they received from *The Black Dwarf* and Cobbett's *Political Register*, from the very radical *Manchester Observer*, and the more middle-class radical journals like the *Leeds Mercury* and *Nottingham Review*, which reported their activities fairly but with mild amusement. The charge of abandonment was countered by the *Manchester Observer*'s defence that they were wives and mothers and by Cobbett's assurance that there was nothing unwomanly or masculine in what they were undertaking.[43] In a spirited defence of the feminist position, Cobbett blasted the women's critics for their stance:

> Just as if women were made for nothing but to cook oatmeal and to sweep a room! Just as if women had no minds! Just as if Hannah More and the Tract Gentry had reduced the women of England to a level with the Negresses of Africa! Just as if England had never had a Queen . . . In all times it is as proper for women as for men, to meddle with public matters.[44]

Cobbett was probably not averse to enlisting the female reformers in the ranks of his admirers, but sometimes the manipulation of women seemed quite blatant. *The Black Dwarf* gave his blessing to the women's cause in 1818, it appeared, in an attempt to rouse the male reformers from their apathy and inertia, and his bantering tone suggested that he was not averse to further exploitation.[45] A month before Peterloo he was prophesying 'And for the SOLDIERS and POLICE OFFICERS, they cannot be arrayed against WOMEN!!! That would be despicable in the extreme.'[46] This kind of patronage they could well have done without. And again, in September 1819, following the arrest of Mrs Wroe, the wife of the editor of the *Manchester Observer*, for selling a radical newspaper, he indulged in a further bout of sexism to taunt his male readers:

> Nothing but the mean dispositions of the local authorities could induce them to harass a woman . . . I am quite sure that the spirit of the brave Lancashire Reformers will not suffer their Lives and their Property, their wives, and their Children to remain long at the disposal of SUCH beings.[47]

Nor were the female reformers themselves unaware of how they were being used. Although they frequently apologised for their femininity and knew that their contributions were not universally welcomed, they were as seriously determined to achieve radical political reform as the male reformers, and they wished to be treated seriously. 'We do not wish for irony and flattery,' wrote one of them; 'We wish you to address our reason.'[48] And Cobbett, for once on the defensive, came back with the assurance that his writings were devoid of anything 'calculated to catch female curiosity and to flatter frivolity and sensuality'.[49]

The desire to be taken seriously and not to be treated in some patronising or light-hearted way because of their gender did not release the female reformers from the need to show why they as women had a particular duty to be involved in the campaign for parliamentary reform and a particular viewpoint to express. Their duty arose from their very role within the home and the family, the suffering they had witnessed and undergone, and their own obligation to attend to the food, the clothing and the domestic well-being of their families, undermined by the economic conditions which they were experiencing. It was their duty and their role, said the Manchester reformers,

to relieve the sufferings of their fellow creatures, from whatever cause they may have arisen. To administer relief to the wretched, to soothe the pains of the distressed, and to pour the balm of consolation upon the wounded in spirit, have ever been considered the appropriate employments of the female sex.[50]

It was defensive and self-deprecating, but it was necessary if their participation was to gain acceptance. Without developing any separate programme for women or drawing attention to their own subjugation, they emphasised those aspects of the reform movement for which they, as women, felt a particular affinity and concern, such as the economic situation that prevailed in working-class homes, the well-being of families, and, especially, their own responsibilities as mothers to educate the next generation in right and proper ideas about the political system and the attitudes that it should engender. The defects and deficiencies of the existing generation were not to be reproduced in the following one.

The extent to which the female reformers were consciously or even subconsciously feminist is not easy to determine. Their declared aims gave little indication of such a position. 'Sharing and sympathizing', said the Blackburn reformers, 'in the pure patriotic feelings of . . . father, brother, or husband', they wished to join with the men in pursuit of the 'hallowed cause' of the restoration of traditional English rights.[51] They accepted male arguments and male purposes, even male myths about lost rights, and it seems inconceivable that their traditional social role and long exclusion from politics could have permitted the instant emergence of a separate political identity and an immediate concern for their own political rights as opposed to those that they sought on behalf of men. Yet the question has been raised of whether women would have gone to the trouble of establishing separate female reform societies just to knit caps of liberty and offer general support for the men's reform movement. Their establishment, it has been argued, expressed a desire for emancipation and was a form of declaration of independence.[52] Women sought and established organisations in which they were not subjected to male domination, and it would be surprising if this, the result of their initiative, were not also one of its intended purposes. This could be a reasonable inference to draw, but the language of the women's campaign is the language of association and co-operation and not that of independence.

Within two months of the formation of the Blackburn Female

Reform Association women had contributed their first martyrs to the cause of parliamentary reform, at Peterloo, Manchester, on 16 August. The female reformers were equally involved with the males in the preparations for the great reform demonstration, preparing their banners and their flags and, presumably, like the men, practising their formations so that they made an orderly and impressive appearance at the meeting. *The Times* correspondent reported that the Oldham female reformers' club of 150 members followed a white silk banner embroidered with the slogan 'Major Cartwright's Bill', 'Annual Parliaments', 'Universal Suffrage' and 'Vote by Ballot' and assumed a position close to the hustings.[53] A similar group from Royton followed two red banners, one carrying demands for the suffrage and parliamentary reform, the other a dramatic exhortation 'Let us DIE like men, and not be SOLD like slaves'.[54] The Middleton contingent, including Bamford and his wife, who came despite her husband's wishes, contained a large number of women:

> At our head were a hundred or two of women, mostly young wives, and mine own was amongst them. — A hundred or two of our handsomest girls — sweethearts to the lads who were with us, — danced to the music, or sung snatches of popular songs.[55]

It was a gala occasion, and the very presence of so many women, in their own ranks or interspersed with the men, was sufficient proof to the *Leeds Mercury* that 'nothing was anticipated that could involve them in the least degree of peril' as they carried their flags and banners surmounted by caps of liberty.[56] One account mentions a group of ten or twelve young women dressed uniformly in white and wearing white caps who were hoisted on to the stage, partly with the help of Henry Hunt himself; 'they appeared to be almost all under twenty, and had rosy interesting faces; they manifested notwithstanding a good share of zeal (despite their faces!) and put on as determined an aspect as their round cheeks could assume'.[57] Another woman in white, Mary Fildes, the President of the Manchester Female Reform Society, rode in Hunt's own carriage, a singular mark of recognition for the women's contribution; she helped unwittingly to create a case of mistaken identity for an unfortunate woman, Elizabeth Gaunt, who was placed in the carriage for protection when she was about to faint and was subsequently kept in solitary confinement for fourteen days before having her case dismissed.[58]

Women were present in force and so it is not surprising that they were prominent among the victims of the outrage. It has been suggested that there were 113 women among the 600 wounded, 14 of them by sabre cuts, and that two women were killed. Immediate reports of the proceedings focused on the women who were cut down and dreadfully wounded:[59] 'Their cries', wrote Bamford, 'were piteous and heart-rending; and would, one might have supposed, have disarmed any human resentment: but here, their appeals were vain. Women, — white-vested maids, and tender youths, were indiscriminately sabred or trampled.'[60]

Bamford's later admission of indiscriminate sabring was at variance with the contemporary suggestion that the yeomen cavalry had deliberately struck against the most defenceless, for 'women seemed special objects of rage of these bastard soldiers'.[61] The affidavit of Elizabeth Farren, standing there out of curiosity and holding her baby, certainly supported the notion that unprovoked personal attacks were made, for she was cut at by a soldier, though standing on the very fringe of the crowd.[62] Bamford's own account mentions a different sort of case of 'a heroine, a young married woman of our party, with her face all bloody, her hair streaming about her, her bonnet hanging by the string, and her apron weighted with stones', who 'kept her assailant at bay until she fell backwards and was near being taken; but she got away covered with severe bruises'.[63]

Attempts by women to expose the conduct of the soldiers after the event led them into further trouble. Sarah Hough was fined £5 at Salford Quarter Sessions, having been charged with political libel, and ordered to be imprisoned until the fine had been paid; Louisa Hough was given a six-month sentence on the same charge; and Lancaster county returns for 1820 showed that thirteen convictions for sedition included one woman, Alice Wroe, of the *Manchester Observer*, who pleaded guilty to publishing a libel on the King's soldiers.[64] Mrs Wroe took up her husband's struggle to sustain an independent and critical newspaper, and her prosecution brought her assistance from the female radical societies. At this time, it was said, working-class papers were often eagerly awaited by women, with children in their arms, who hoped that the week-end reading matter would arrive promptly on Saturday to help keep the man of the family at home and out of the local pub.[65] The demands of female radicals for better education for their children and themselves suggest that many would themselves be avid readers of such literature and welcome it for its own sake.

Samuel Bamford, having been sheltered by 'an old female reformer', eventually found himself on the way to York to face treason charges, accompanied again by determined women from the ranks of the female reformers.[66] They also continued to appear in force to greet Hunt whenever he appeared, in Manchester or in London, but their place in the history of the parliamentary reform and working-class movements had already been guaranteed by their apearance on the field of Peterloo, hereafter an evocative name of unequalled potency, recalling a time

> When infants, borne in starving mothers' arms,
> Unlawful wounded by infernal arms;
> Thus eager, fame to gain — nor sex, nor age,
> Nor friend, escap'd the madness of their rage.[67]

Peterloo did not mark the end of women's involvement in this phase of the reform movement. The protests and the prosecutions continued, and when Hunt re-emerged from prison he still commanded a great personal following. On 13 November 1822, women from local branches of the Great Northern Union joined a procession in Rochdale on behalf of Hunt and this latest attempt to rally the forces of reform, but the momentum was temporarily lost.[68]

A different issue served in 1820 – 1 as a focal point for women's political protest and that was the case of Queen Caroline, whose alleged persecution by her husband and the government created a popular cause that could be exploited by Opposition Whig politicians and had, at the same time, a deprived woman at its centre. Whatever the personal merits of the Queen, she evoked a popular response from the still organised working-class groups of the large towns, including Manchester, Blackburn, Leeds, Bradford, Newcastle and Leicester. Addresses of sympathy were presented to her and signatures collected on her behalf; there were even collections of money made to which only women were allowed to contribute in the evident belief that an important feminist principle was at stake.[69] A popular heroine permitted extensive publicity to and discussion of the glorious deeds of women through the ages, and the two-way correspondence between the Queen and the women of England encouraged a mutual love affair which produced glowing tributes on both sides. The women of Newcastle, for instance, addressed the Queen as 'wives, mothers, and daughters' and proclaimed the wrongs of an innocent woman and injured wife and the Queen's acts of enlightened benevolence.[70] Caroline's 'blessed' status among women was their inspiration for renewed determination to instil right political notions into their children's minds, a reinforcement of the previous campaign's theme, and for her part the Queen was not averse to making references to the 'sacred principles of the Constitution', the need for a free press, and the government's many acts of outrage in suppressing popular rights. She also made reference to the 'superior degree of intellectual cultivation' demonstrated by the women who had espoused her cause, a recognition of their recent successes in moving into the political sphere and conducting political arguments and political campaigns.[71]

It is interesting to note that while the Queen Caroline affair gave further encouragement to newer forms of political expression and behaviour, it did at the same time provoke responses of a more traditional kind. On 7 July 1820, for example, the town clerk of Dover reported to the Home Secretary on the unpleasant circumstances that had arisen following the arrival of ten foreigners who had landed in England to give evidence against the Queen. Their coming had received some publicity, and an assembled crowd of the 'lower orders', men and women, had 'manifested a most improper and violent disposition towards them'. So great was the turmoil that they had been unable to leave their inn and the London coach had had to leave without them. A woman called Thomsett was subsequently apprehended and charged with having struck one of the foreigners in the face.[72] The Home Secretary was thus receiving confirmation that the ways of old England had not completely changed as well as the more ominous news that 2,000 or so women had been present at a public meeting in Leeds; they deeply deplored the abuse of the Queen; 'at the same time', they said, 'would drop the tear of Sympathy with you as wives, mothers, and as Daughters'. Women they remained, despite their new-found interest in politics.[73]

The years between the Queen Caroline affair and the events associated with the passing of the Great Reform Bill have traditionally been regarded as a quiet period between two of intense activity, the 'quiescent twenties' that came between decades when far more happened in the history of radicalism and the growth of women's political involvement. The picture still remains broadly the same, but attention has recently been drawn to one series of developments at least which was important both for radicalism and for women, namely that associated with the so-called Zetetic, or radical free thought, movement of Richard Carlile.[74] This writer, who had denounced sexual inequality, was imprisoned in 1820, and his journal, *The Republican*, was saved by the rallying to the cause of his wife Jane and his sister Mary Ann. But this was no ordinary case of a family compensating for the absence of its male head, for with the trial of Jane on a charge of seditious libel for material published in *The Republican* on 16 June 1820, and her conviction and imprisonment for two years, a much greater effort was required. Susannah Wright, a Nottingham lace-maker, volunteered to come to London to take charge of the publishing house, and was herself imprisoned for selling Carlile's pamphlets, a 'wretched and shameless woman', an 'abandoned creature' according to some.[75] Women kept the venture going by their support at all levels. The wives of the shopmen who produced the paper took responsibility for its distribution and sale, and offers of help from provincial centres kept pace with the prosecutions endured by this devoted band of women helpers through to 1827. During this time the London-based organisation maintained an enthusiastic correspondence with female republican societies in the old organisational centres such as Manchester, Blackburn, Ashton, Bolton and Bath, which provided the subscriptions necessary to keep the persecuted journal alive. The Carlile supporters, identified as the wives of shopkeepers, skilled labourers and artisans, or industrial workers in their own right, were in part acting out of necessity, selling books and papers, collecting money, preparing food for their imprisoned husbands, and managing families, but they were at the same time, it is argued, developing a feminine consciousness and contributing notably to the cause of women's emancipation. Susannah Wright, for instance, made strong demands for educational rights for women and full participation in the cultural benefits society could offer. Although there is no suggestion that the women associated with Carlile were anything other than a small number of very determined and courageous free-thinking political radicals, whose ideas on religion and sex would certainly have precluded them from having great popular influence, they do represent an important women's achievement in these years and certainly reveal women in something more than an auxiliary or support role.

The re-opening of the great debate on parliamentary reform in

1830 seems to have aroused women's interest again, but the women's role is not so clearly marked out in 1830 – 2 as it was in 1819. Women were still enthusiastically mobilising to chair Hunt following his election for Preston in December 1830, processing arm in arm and carrying radical banners.[76] And the women of Manchester, under their President, Hannah Brooks, and Secretary, Ann Foster, had their own Female Radical Reform Society, which they reconstituted as a branch of the National Union of Working Classes, pursuing a programme of manhood suffrage, annual parliaments and the ballot.[77] There were female political unions in Hyde, Heywood and other manufacturing areas, but there is little evidence of any great expansion of organisations since the days of 1819.[78] The number of specifically female societies was either not great or else the lack of novelty on this occasion caused their activities to be less newsworthy. Also, the major unions were now happy to welcome women as members. The constitution of the Birmingham Political Union declared that membership was to be open to all persons, and the National Union of Working Classes followed suit.[79] At a meeting in October 1831, Mr Cleave moved a resolution:

That at future meetings of the Union at Rotunda, the wives of members be admitted free of expense. (Cheers)

His reasons for so doing do not stand up to feminist scrutiny; he thought that meetings would be ornamented by women's presence; he was satisfied that there would be more peace and happiness at home; he was aware that women in general were Tories but if they could be induced to attend there they would shortly become republicans and would then raise the next generation to be different from the slaves of the existing one.[80] If men really were keen to have women's help in the cause of parliamentary reform, this mixture of patronage, flattery, insult and cajoling seems hardly the most appropriate way of attracting it, but there is little evidence to suggest that this kind of appeal evoked great hostility.

During 1831 the Reform crisis helped to precipitate a series of riots in England and Wales. After the Carmarthen election of 1831 a riot occurred during which Anne Jones threw a stone which struck the newly elected winner, but this act was trivial compared with the activities of women during the Merthyr riots.[81] They are said to have formed a large part of the vocal crowds and to have jeered the Argyll and Sutherland Highlanders with taunts that they should go home and put their trousers on. They were also involved in some pillaging of shops, carrying off sides of bacon and other provisions. For these offences, two women received twelve months' hard labour; the judge informed them that they should not be spared on account of their sex in view of the active part which they had played in the riots.[82] At the other notorious disturbances of 1831, the October riots in Nottingham and Bristol, their part is more obscure. It is inconceivable that there were no women in the great crowds that gathered in Nottingham Market Place on 10 October prior to the events which culminated in the firing of the castle. But their presence certainly rated no particular mention, and in the 33 people who were later arrested in connection with the disturbances women featured not at all.[83] In Bristol the first reports of the much more serious disturbances there suggested that one woman had been killed and a few injured, and a slightly later report indicated that 60 people, men, women and children, had been arrested for plunder.[84] Shortly afterwards an Irish woman charged with rioting was found to have two silk waistcoats and two blankets wrapped around her waist and pretended to be 'as ladies would wish to be'.[85] These scraps of information do, however, tell us nothing about the political behaviour of the women of Nottingham and Bristol during the crisis.

The most important development of this period was the formation in London in July 1832 of a female society 'The Friends of the Oppressed' 'to aid and assist the wives and families of those who suffer in the people's cause', which, its members hoped, would 'call forth the latent courage of their husbands, brothers, and sweethearts . . . in the glorious contest of RIGHT against MIGHT'.[86] They gave support, moral and financial, to the families of political prisoners, especially those involved in the struggle for the free press, and acted in close association with the National Union of Working Classes in the London area. At their public meetings they displayed a 'chaste and unassuming manner', doubtless felt to be appropriate to working men's wives, and their colleagues in other parts of the country also accepted limitations in the extent of their role.[87] M.A.B., from Bristol, having seen in the *Poor Man's Guardian* a proposal that shopkeepers belonging to the Political Union should have their names published so that other members could deal with them, was inspired to write: 'this is what women can do . . . without a moment's neglect of our ordinary occupations.

The spending of money (especially in domestic concerns) is the province of women, in it we can act without the risk of being called politicians.'[88] Exclusive dealing, practised as early as 1820 in Oldham, was evidently considered by M.A.B. to be an acceptable woman's technique, more sophisticated than food rioting, but still within the woman's sphere and not likely to incur accusations about politics.[89] The limitations of M.A.B.'s thinking and her ambitions for women were summed up in her concluding sentence, when she argued: 'Men of sense will not love us less for having talent, provided we use it right and for their benefit.' And the right way to use it was in 'consoling our husbands under their privations, strengthening their hands and invigorating their minds for the carrying on of the noble work already begun'.[90] Similarly, the Manchester female reformers 'being mothers, daughters, sisters, and relatives to those who have been for a long time struggling for liberty, feel it our duty to render them a helping hand at this momentous crisis; seeing as we do daily, our children on the brink of starvation owing to profligate government'.[91]

It is ironical that, at a time when some women believed that they had a duty to come to the aid of the male reformers, the *Poor Man's Guardian* was examining the reasons why women were, in the editor's view, indifferent, or even hostile, to reform. They are not without interest; women disliked politics in general because they caused men to neglect their wives and homes and women were soon discouraged if they saw no prospect of quick success. The prescribed remedy was for men to avoid public houses, make their meetings shorter, and persuade their wives that they had nothing to lose and everything to gain by parliamentary reform.[92] Wherever the real apathy, it is interesting that some men were now thinking about women's attitudes and that the support of women was evidently considered to be worth having.

In one area women remained very much to the forefront of a radical campaign — the struggle for a free press, in which the Friends of the Oppressed continued the traditions of the Carlile supporters in the twenties. When this organisation was established by London women in July 1832, they expressed as one of their central aims 'support of a really free and untaxed press' and war against 'the perpetration of the most atrocious cruelties against the poor men, for merely vending cheap knowledge'.[93] The *Poor Man's Guardian* both publicised the activities and was itself in need of their assistance, for many of the people whom the Society helped were being punished for their association with the *Guardian*. The newspaper was not averse to exploiting the fact that a public meeting to be held on 14 August 'in aid of the Wives and Children of the Men confined in Lancaster Castle' would be 'entirely conducted by females' and thereby would ensure an overflow of attenders because of the novelty of the proceedings.[94] The Society advertised for cases needing relief to be brought to their attention, and they assisted victims of all kinds of persecution.[95] In December 1832, for instance, their beneficiaries were 'the victims of the rural tyranny of the farmer-overseers of Chilbolton, near Winchester', people who had allegedly been denied poor relief because of their membership of the National Union of Working Classes, but frequently the free press campaign was uppermost.[96] In October 1832, a group of about one hundred women, described as 'a few of our members', assembled to welcome back May Willis, who had spent fourteen days in the House of Correction for selling the *Poor Man's Guardian*, and the 'intrepid old lady' was placed at the head of their procession.[97] In December they met to consider further means of supporting Mr Hetherington in the holy cause of liberty';[98] some doubtless decided that one way of doing so was to respond to E. Hancock's appeal to 'The Female Radicals and Republicans of London'; he proposed opening a school in 1833 in response to the wishes of 'a great number of his female Radical friends'. Children would not be debarred from reading 'any book of a moral tendency', though no religious doctrine was to be taught. The *Poor Man's Guardian* was to be weekly reading and 'every thing requisite to make them ardent friends of liberty, and rational members of society'.[99] There would presumably be no restriction on T. Larkin's *Sermon to Soldiers*, based on the text 'Do violence to no man,' which Hetherington and other booksellers, including Mrs Mann of Leeds, were currently retailing.[100]

The Friends of the Oppressed, though clearly departing a great distance from the paths that women were supposed to tread at this time, were not strident in their independence. They even managed to use prevailing notions of the feminine stereotype to their own advantage when they asked: 'What course will the dastardly and contemptible Whigs now adopt? Will they add to the cruelty and injustice inflicted daily upon the destitute cripples and starving old men by entering upon a war against Petticoats?'[101] The question was partially answered in the affirmative when prosecutions were brought against women as well as against men, and here again women found some advantage in exploiting the stereotype. When, for instance, Mrs Wastneys of Newcastle was imprisoned for six months in May 1834 for selling illegal newspapers, the frailty of her sex was pleaded as an extenuating circumstance that should be considered when her sentence was awarded.[102] As other governments were to discover on later occasions, there were certain inherent disadvantages in a contest involving women on the opposite side.

The prevailing impression of the early decades of the nineteenth century is of a period in which women made their first appearances on the political scene with a purpose of assisting men in their campaigns. It is no insult to the female activists of these times to label their role as an auxiliary one; rather is it a tribute to their selflessness to note that they were more concerned to know what they could do for others than to attempt to agitate on their own behalf. This view does not ignore the existence of the occasional woman such as Susannah Wright, who, it has been argued, was possessed of a 'militant, sophisticated, feminist consciousness' by 1825.[103] It simply recognises that the vast majority of the women who were politically involved, and altogether they were, of course, no more than a tiny minority of all women, did not demand rights for women but sometimes rights for people and often rights for men. If there was an implicit demand for recognition and for equality in their very participation, this was rarely made explicit. Rather did women present themselves with reluctance and apology and almost always on behalf of their men. This does not mean that the question of women's rights was not raised. The presence of women in politics made this inevitable. The ambiguity of the term 'universal suffrage' and the readiness of most people to equate it with 'manhood suffrage' inevitably prompted the minority to point out that 'universal' might conceivably be interpreted as including women. Some used this to demonstrate the total folly of the radical case, for no one, it was argued, could possibly suppose that women should be given the vote. That could even lead to the unthinkable proposition that women might be allowed to sit in Parliament and participate in the legislative process.[104] When faced with this kind of debate, serious or comic according to the disposition of the writer or his concept of what constituted humour, some radicals were driven to reply, 'And why not?' Some felt that the case for widows and spinsters was easy to make, since a woman who lacked a husband to speak for her was felt to have more need for the opportunity to protect her own interests; after all, women were not disqualified from succession to the throne. Others accepted that there was no moral difference between the sexes and that universal suffrage must mean what it said. And no less a person than Jeremy Bentham was ready to admit that he saw no reason why women should not share in the elective franchise.[105] William Thompson, in his 1825 *Appeal to One Half of the Human Race, Women, Against the Pretensions of the Other Half, Men*, argued that only by participating in government could women's grievances be removed, but the lack of enthusiasm for this proposition amongst men was not balanced by any compensatory zeal on women's part that this should occur. In the columns of *Crisis*, 'Concordia' argued that women should be able to legislate for themselves, but Robert Owen, to whom she was directing her address, replied: 'I still fear there are not yet so much general knowledge and moral courage in the women as are necessary to enable them to legislate for themselves with full advantage.'[106] It was a discouraging reply, though Owen had little enthusiasm for a working-class franchise anyway, and it has been argued that women always had a greater degree of equality with men within Owenite schemes than they did outside them, whatever Owen's position on the vote.[107] Despite the initiatives of a few women who followed Carlile or debated with Owen, there was little in this period to suggest the making of the English female consciousness or to identify many women ready to fulfil the destiny sketched out by 'Caroline' of Pimlico in 1818 when she had forecast a role for women outside the nursery and inside the very halls of state.[108]

6 CHARTIST WOMEN

Just as Chartism was the first working-class political movement that was truly national in scope, so too was it the first political movement that involved women from all over England, Scotland and Wales in their tens of thousands. The reform movement of 1819 had interested small numbers of women from a few areas of England, the anti-Poor Law movement had brought in greater numbers over a bigger geographical area on the one specific issue; but Chartism, besides increasing numbers enormously and securing nation-wide participation, also focused attention as no other movement had ever done on the whole social and economic structure of the country and its relationship to politics. In this examination women played an important part, as people, as workers, and as women. Its importance is not to be measured by the attention paid to women's participation in standard histories of Chartism, for they have indeed largely ignored the issue, but is none the less indicated by the innumerable women's organisations that came into existence during the Chartist movement and their contributions to the great debate.

The emergence of women as determined Chartists in 1838 was no eruption of self-confident females looking for fresh fields to conquer and moving with enthusiasm into the new sphere of politics. Women had been too long and too unquestioningly excluded from politics for this to be possible, and when they came into politics they came in with the certain knowledge that this was a departure from their traditional role and would be so regarded. They explained this change, not in terms of discontent with their previous lot but in their inability any longer to sustain it. Had they possessed any choice, they said, their preference would have been to avoid politics and seek the quiet domestic existence which society had ordained for them, but the options, they believed, were closing. The Stockport Chartists of 1839 declared:

> We regret that we should be driven by dire necessity to depart from the limits usually prescribed for female duties; but when ... we find it impossible to discharge those duties in our relative capacities — when even with the most rigid economy we are

111

unable to provide for the actual necessities of subsistence . . . we feel justified in declaring our conviction that nothing less than the adoption of the principles of the People's Charter can effectually remove the existing distress, or secure the safety of the working classes.[1]

Domestic duties were not being shirked. As the Female Political Union of Newcastle declared in February 1839:

For years we have struggled to maintain our homes in comfort, such as our hearts told us should greet our husbands after their fatiguing labours. Year after year has passed away, and even now our wishes have no prospect of being realised, our husbands are over wrought, our houses half-furnished, our families ill-fed and our children uneducated.

And the cause of these evils, they said, was the fact that the government of the country was in the hands of the 'upper and middle classes, while the working men who form the millions, the strength and wealth of the country, are left without the pale of the Constitution'.[2] Therefore, declared the London Female Democratic Association 'even woman, domesticated woman, leaving her homestead, will battle for the rights of those that are dear to her.' Some would argue, declared the Keighley Female Radical Association in October 1839, that it was not the business of women to interfere in politics; that had been their view, but when their children were starving they believed that it was the duty of all working men and women to express their political sentiments publicly and publicise their wants and grievances.[4] Women would not have been interested in politics if they had not suffered by politics.

This was the message, restrained, defensive, almost apologetic, but still pointing to a clear link between the role prescribed for them, the reasons why this could not be properly fulfilled, and the reasons which now prompted them towards politics as the remaining option. The existing system of government, said the women of Brampton, was 'alike unwise, impolitic, and unjust'.[5] 'We entreat you', therefore, said those of Newcastle, 'to join us to help the cause of freedom, justice, honesty, and truth, to drive poverty and ignorance from our land, and establish happy homes, true religion, righteous government, and good laws.'[6]

Nor was justice or righteous government to be achieved with the assistance of the established political parties or within the frame-

work of parliamentary politics as then constituted. The misgovernment of the Whigs and the Tories was attacked as the political
cause of the miserable working-class condition, and the accusation
was quite specifically made that existing government represented
class interests opposed to those of the working classes from which
the female Chartists came. The Northampton Female Radical
Association, for instance, condemned 'the wretched and degraded
condition of the working classes, which 'we are convinced arises
from an unjust system of legislation';[7] the Sheffield Female
Chartist Association spoke of 'starving thousands' and declared its
opposition to 'the despotism of class legislation';[8] Mary Ann
Walker, speaking of the plight of the female shirt-makers in
London, attacked 'class legislation'.[9] Such declarations contain
more explicit references to class and a more complete awareness or
consciousness of class than are to be found in earlier periods, and
they matched anything that the men's leaders had to say on this
subject.

Nor were the women willing to separate any longer the issues of
political rights and working-class poverty. Where the two had been
linked in 1819 the assumption had been that taxation and borough-
mongering were responsible for the working-class plight. Now, by
contrast, the women of the Bristol Female Patriotic Association,
addressing their 'Sisters' of the West of England and South Wales,
did so in terms of the low men's wages that were driving women out
to work and the need for 'a fair day's wages for a fair day's
work'.[10] They were voicing Harold Perkin's working-class ideal in
opposition to a middle-class ethic that labour must be obtained at
the lowest possible price.[11] The desperation with existing living
conditions, with starving children and downtrodden husbands, was
now evoking something more than the traditional direct action of
economic protest, such as food rioting. It was producing political
protest directed against a whole system believed to be operating on
behalf of class interests and needing to be radically reformed so
that other interests might be accommodated.

If female Chartists were insistent that they would never have quit
their homes for the meeting rooms unless their homes had been
under threat, they were equally consistent in their argument that
they came into politics to support their men, not to supersede them
or in any way to rival them. The argument was another extension of
the process of rationalisation by which they were able to show that
their movement into politics, far from being a perversion of their

natural role, was rather a fulfilment of it. Woman was man's help-mate, and so it was incumbent upon her to come to his assistance, even in this somewhat unaccustomed matter of helping him to win the vote. Although there was a fondness for citing the feats of historical heroines who had supported what were thought to be noble causes, Joan of Arc, Flora MacDonald, Charlotte Cordé, for example, few statements suggested that the female Chartists aspired to this kind of role.[12] Rather was the auxiliary role the chosen one. This was a self-imposed limitation on the female contribution, which has disappointed some historians, but it characterised many of their pronunciations. The Ashton Female Political Union enjoined its members: 'Remember, dear Sisters, what glorious auxiliaries the friends of the human race have had amongst our sex,' and other groups struck the same note.[13] The Rochdale Female Radical Society resolved to assist their husbands, fathers and brothers to work out their political salvation or fall in the attempt.

The 'incessant support and able advocacy of the working man's rights' was the undertaking of the Hull Female Patriotic Association, and the Female Radical Association of Sheffield felt a positive obligation to perform such a service, for it insisted that it was 'the duty of all females who respect themselves or their sex — who have any regard for their husbands, or love for their children, or sympathy with their countrymen, now to come forward and co-operate'.[15] It was an auxiliary, even a subservient, role that the women accepted, but there was an element of calculation, cunning even, in the way it was exercised, for Susannah Inge, the energetic leader of the City of London, advised her followers that by participating in the political activities which most pleased their Chartist fathers and husbands, they would be an inspiration to them and 'urge them to further exertions'.[16] A little prompting, she supposed, might achieve a lot.

Not only was the support of the men a duty to be done; it was also a righteous cause to be upheld. The whole experience of women, argued Thomas Clutton Salt of Birmingham, their suffering, their married life, their motherhood, their religious fervour, and their radical patriotism encouraged and required them 'to join the holy league of righteousness and love', 'to recover the promises of abundance God has made to the diligent'.[17] If this was to be the inspiration of women's participation in Chartism, it was important that the numerous females who assembled to hear Henry

Vincent in Bristol in 1838 should have been 'well-dressed', and that the rules and regulations of the Barnsley group should have required

> That no disorderly person be admitted in the room during the transaction of business, any one creating disturbance, to be turned out; and that all members of the Union pay obedience to the Chairwoman of the evening, when called to order, or requested to keep silence, or to be turned out of the room.[18]

Determination and respectability were keynotes of women's politics, and especially when they were in pursuit of righteousness.

It is not difficult to understand how readily many women imagined a religious sanction for what they were undertaking, for 'What are politics, but an important branch of morals, relating to our duty to our neighbours?' asked the female reformers of Bath.[19] In fulfilling this duty they found a moral defence of their political behaviour, which became a series of 'hallowed endeavours' and 'sacred duties', justified by the Biblical texts which came easily to their tongues and their pens. Their speeches and writings often reveal an evangelical familiarity with Scriptures, and it seems not unreasonable to suppose that a chapel background probably helped to develop in some of the Chartist women those qualities and abilities frequently associated with Nonconformist religion: an experience and love of equality; talents of leadership; the power to use words. Such attributes translated readily to the political scene, especially when, as sometimes happened, the Chartist meeting was held in the local chapel or based on the style of the Camp Meeting in the open air.[20]

It was not thought unnatural to sing Methodist or other hymns on these occasions. The Bradford women concluded their meeting of late January 1839 with the radical hymn 'Rise, ye people!', which would hardly have been to the taste of John Wesley, and at Hull, in July, a hymn was followed by a prayer 'imploring the Great Creator of the Universe to protect and assist their glorious cause'.[21] Inspired by the scriptures, women sought to realise by political actions their spiritual hopes of freedom and other desired ends. The Whigs and Tories were quite simply 'anti-christian', as Chartist women found a whole collection of texts which seemed properly applicable to their own mission.[22] Physical force sentiments were supported by the words ''Tis better to be slain by the sword than die with hunger' or Ruth's famous utterance to

Naomi, suitably extended by the Thornley women, 'Whither thou goest I will go' even if it were to the mouth of the cannon.[23] Virtually every facet of the female Chartists' campaign received such unimpeachable Biblical sanction, especially after some slight manipulation or adjustment to suit the women's political objectives. At the radical demonstration at Colne, in October 1838, women's banners were particularly strong on religious texts such as the reminder that 'Whoso stoppeth his ears at the cry of the poor he also shall cry himself, but shall not be heard.'[24] Similarly at Nottingham, on 5 November, women's banners proclaimed:

Why grind ye the faces of the poor saith the Lord.
Freedom's cause cannot be lost,
It is sacred before the Lord of Hosts.[25]

Not surprisingly, Chartism found some support in the women's temperance societies of the late 1830s and early 1840s, for 'No government', proclaimed the East London Female Temperance Society in 1841, 'can long withstand the just claims of a people who have courage to conquer their own vices.'[26] The relationship between the temperance and Chartist movements seems rather ambiguous, but it was evidently strong enough to justify the *Northern Star* as well as *The English Chartist Circular*, the latter committed to upholding both causes, giving full reports to organisations that opposed the consumption of alcohol and tobacco. Self-denial of these two commodities was also a denial of revenue from taxation to the authorities whom the Chartists opposed; and the man and woman who set the example of abstinence to their children would be better fitted, because free of vice, to lead a righteous cause and to accept the responsibilities of power once the struggle was over. Meanwhile they added a note of moral rectitude and integrity to the campaigns of many female Chartists and helped to assuage the criticism that women with political ideas were frivolous.

Another attempt to rationalise the involvement of women in Chartism was the importance which they ascribed to their own position as educators of the rising generation. Sophia of Birmingham, a prolific writer on Chartism and women's part in the movement, grimly told her readers that her own parents, she supposed, would never have taught her to read and write had they imagined that she might become a Chartist, but she saw it as her function, and that of other women, for the future to ensure that children were brought up with a proper understanding of certain vital matters:

> let us as Chartist women and mothers, instruct and encourage each other, that our children shall be better informed of their rights as citizens, that their morals be of a higher order; and that, when the time arrives, when they should receive those rights, they shall be better prepared by the training received from their mothers to enjoy them.[27]

The acceptance of female responsibility for the formation of infant minds and the provision of a radical education for future generations of workers meant acceptance of the social stereotype role for themselves. At the same time, women were not only legitimising their involvement in politics; they were also making a clear declaration of intent to go on ensuring that the ideas that were currently being debated would continue to be handed on to their children. And to do that they needed to go beyond the stereotype, for to be educators they needed themselves to be educated. Though literate herself, Sophia implored the men to 'throw open the doors of learning to us, and permit us to enter'. Women must demonstrate their 'eagerness to abandon frivolities and seek knowledge', without, of course, neglecting domestic duties.[28] If they were to be taken seriously, they must behave seriously. If they wished to overcome old male prejudices which had militated powerfully against female improvement and political involvement in the past, women should prove their intellectual capacity and thereby achieve equality with men in political activity. As women had been 'the best advocates for Liberty' in all ages, argued the Elland Female Radical Association, they must both give and receive instruction in political knowledge.[29] And so, when the Gorbals Female Universal Suffrage Association framed its working rules in December 1839, it laid down that in cases where meetings ended at nine o'clock and members had an hour to spare,

> the remaining hour shall be devoted to reading instructive essays, or extracts from popular works, chiefly upon political subjects; also short addresses from the members of the Committee of Guardians, or from any of the females, in order to instruct each other in political and scientific subjects, the more effectually to

spread useful knowledge, and thereby progress eventually to the People's Charter.[30]

In many ways the statement was a classic piece of earnest Victorian self-improvement, but for women. If the starting-point of this aspect of the women's case was the social stereotype woman, responsible for forming infant minds through her role in mother-hood, the finishing point appeared to be a race of politically literate females some way removed from the Victorian ideal. Nor would the males be left behind if they agreed to follow the suggestion of T. B. Smith of Leeds, who proposed Chartist Sunday Schools 'open for the reception of both children and adults of both sexes, and without reference to any sectarian religious creed'.[31]

Not every female Chartist accepted this kind of proposition. Miss Lennox of the Gorbals would have had no relish for the extra hour's instruction, for she believed that politics should form no great part in female education, thereby exacerbating the difficulties of her co-Chartists who felt constantly obliged to explain and defend their unnatural political intervention.[32] Usually, like the women of Stockport, they accepted that the domestic role was the normal and natural one, and even Sophia of Birmingham confessed her belief that women were best at home, but argued that when mis-government made that role intolerable they had to step forward and do something about it.[33] But they did it apologetically, not in defiance but with regret, like Mary Ann Moore, one of the Female Radicals of Perth, who presented scarves to visiting male speakers with the words 'Gentlemen, we have no desire to appear con-spicuous before the world' and an assurance that they had no personal ambition to gratify.[34] When they did, in spite of everything, appear conspicuous before the world, they knew that their conduct would come under the closest scrutiny. Sophia, dis-cussing the problems confronting women in politics, explained the price to be paid: 'We are careful that our houses be more clean, our children better instructed, our own persons scrupulously neat; and, that, when in conversation, they are gratified to perceive our taste improved, and never turn a frowning reproof upon any inattention to domestic comfort.'[35]

But with all these difficulties facing them, women still had the best precedent in the world for a political role 'as it is a female that assumes to rule this nation in defiance of the universal rights of man and woman'.[36] This argument, of the London Female

Democratic Association, seemed to imply that what Queen Victoria could withold or take away, that would the women of Britain restore.

Nowhere are the difficulties of the female Chartists more in evidence than in their treatment by men, who produced every kind of response to their political involvement. Many of the male Chartist leaders were very enthusiastic in their support for women; Henry Vincent made a speciality of addressing women's meetings: less flamboyant, Thomas Clutton Salt of Birmingham appears to have been the first man to aim specifically at recruiting their support. By a programme of rousing lectures in his home town in the summer of 1838 he launched the Birmingham Female Chartist Association, perhaps the largest of all the women's groups, and he toured the industrial north during that year stressing the value of female support for Chartism and encouraging women to become involved. As early as May 1838, Salt had declared unequivocally that the male Chartists could afford neither their hostility nor even their neutrality; 'they must be our enthusiastic friends.'[37] It became increasingly believed that unless women became convinced of the need for the Charter, their natural conservatism would cause them to impede the democratic cause; if a universal object was to be achieved, ran one argument, the surest way was to enlist the sympathies and quicken the intellects of wives and children.[38] Men's support for them was therefore a matter of principle and expediency. No doubt O'Connor, Vincent and other public orators were much flattered to address receptive audiences of women, but others, like Bronterre O'Brien, were more ready to argue the principle involved. Women, argued O'Brien, suffered just as much as men from bad government, which was equally destructive to the rights and happiness of both sexes; they paid the same taxes; they were punished by the same laws; and they performed more than half the drudgery of life.[39]

Yet not all leaders were sensitive to these considerations. It was a later expressed regret of Ernest Jones that more attention had not been paid to women and children, whom he described as 'the key to working class progress', and when women were invited, apparently unequivocally, to co-operate with men, there was often a sting in the tail of the invitation.[40] In September 1842, for instance, there was an appeal by the male Chartists of London to the women of the capital to 'Come . . . and assist us in the holy work, for you can do much to strengthen us'; the reward for such co-operation was that 'it will place you on a better, more equal footing with man, and will render you more valuable, more endearing to those to whom God has given you, as his choicest gift, his greatest blessing.'[41] Such an appeal would scarcely have gladdened the hearts of such feminists as had emerged by this stage.

In fact there was a fairly general tendency for male Chartists to exploit their female supporters, consciously or unconsciously, throughout their relationship. The very concept of supporters, which the women prescribed for themselves, almost implied a willingness to be exploited, but this occurred with varying degrees of tact and diplomacy. In February 1838, when the women of Elland were still accepting addresses from male speakers, they were flatteringly told that they were the best politicians, the best revolutionaries and the best political economists, which they doubtless believed or disbelieved according to their dispositions, for these tributes were not unduly patronising.[42] The women of Leicester, however, were told of the importance of the 'presence and smiles of the ladies', and those of Calton and Mile End Universal Suffrage Associations were similarly assured that 'The pleasant smiles of the ladies, and the rougher, though not less hearty plaudits of the males could not but encourage and gratify the speakers.'[43] The presence of women at political meetings was frequently welcomed for decorative reasons, but the exploitation could take subtler forms. Women were alleged to be defenceless creatures who would be exploited unless males came to their protection, by supporting the Charter, and William Lovett himself used the argument that women were being degraded as the victims of a corrupt system, which therefore needed to be reformed.[44] A more overt exploitation of sex occurred, on this occasion by women themselves, in the declaration of the Ashton Political Union that 'he that is willing to live a slave deserves not the smiles of a lady,' whilst Caroline, a young factory worker in *Sybil*, declared her resolution never to marry 'any man who is not for the Five Points'.[45] Inevitably this theme was too good for the men themselves to resist. Julian Harney, for instance, advocated at Newcastle in June 1839 that women should bestow their favours selectively according to the political persuasions of the males. Rather than face life without a sweetheart, some uncommitted working men might of necessity have first embraced Chartist principles and then the women who supported them; 'Soon the young men would be most uproarious Democrats,' said Harney, 'and soon the young women would have sweethearts enough.'[46]

It is, in fact, impossible to resist the view that some of the Chartist leaders found themselves, unwittingly or otherwise, the focal point of a good deal of female affection. The women's societies frequently expressed their fervent admiration for the male speakers who addressed them, O'Connor, Frost, Harney and Vincent, for example, and were always ready to pay strong tribute to what they called the patriotism of these men, a useful word which could mean whatever people wished it to mean. The extravagant praise unfailingly bestowed upon certain male speakers and the dramatic pledges of support made by the women suggest that some women could well have been attracted by the glamour of radical heroes rather than their political aims and programmes. This was no new thing, for Henry Hunt had found himself the centre of such adulation in the days before and after Peterloo. Now it was Feargus O'Connor who, on his release from York Castle, could bring out the ladies of Leeds 'who had been prompted by curiosity and the fineness of the day to witness the ceremonial', for it evidently did not occur to the *Leeds Intelligencer* that women could have attended the political function for its own sake. At a meeting shortly afterwards in the same city, there were again present 'numbers of well dressed females . . . whose presence seemed to furnish great inducement to order in the rougher sex'. O'Connor thanked 'some ladies who had presented him with a huge rosette suspended from a broad green ribbon inscribed "Universal Suffrage" and "No Surrender", and toasts were drunk to "The Ladies" '.[47]

It was not, however, Feargus O'Connor but Henry Vincent who was the real darling of the female Chartists:

> With the fair sex his slight handsome figure, the merry twinkle of his eye, his incomparable mimicry, his passionate burst of enthusiasm, the rich music of his voice, and above all, his appeals for the elevation of woman, rendered him a universal favourite.[48]

Vincent, it is said, always had an eye on his adoring female audience and conceded that he never saw a more gratifying sight than the 'pretty lasses' who came along to listen to him. Whether it was with the 'large and attentive meetings of the ladies of Hull', or the ever grateful ladies of Trowbridge, who presented him with a green scarf and a handsome suit of clothes, Vincent could be sure of a good reception from his female listeners.[49]

Female Chartists could not, of course, expect a good reception from all the men whose positions caused them to feel obliged to pass judgement on their behaviour. Newspaper editors were one such category, and many were inclined to treat women with insufferable patronage or disparaging comment. The presence of women at political meetings was often taken as an indication of the meeting's relative failure, for reports would contain the damning reference to the fact that a large proportion of the crowd or audience was made up of women or, equally frequently, 'women and boys'. The *Leeds Intelligencer* combined this approach with the condescending advice to its readers that they should allow their wives to start reading newspapers.[50] *The Age* and *The Satirist* ridiculed the idea of women's involvement in political agitation, but *The Times* was the most ferocious in its condemnation. In October 1842, in reporting some meetings that had taken place in Manchester, it labelled the female Chartists as 'freaks', calling their actions strange, absurd, inane, disgraceful, disgusting and, above all, 'destructive of the best feelings of humanity'. Ideas of women's suffrage, or even women's rights to interest themselves in men's suffrage, it subjected to the strongest mockery and ridicule, drawing again upon the social stereotype of the woman with sacred female duties as helpmate, mother and housekeeper, which were now irresponsibly neglected.[51] This reasoning again illustrates why women were so concerned to demonstrate that their political interest arose, legitimately, from this very same domestic context. *The Times*' jibe which appears to have been most wounding, certainly most quoted, was that of 'Hen Chartists'.

Punch had its own approach to the question in 1848, when it delivered a blatantly sexist attack in an article entitled 'How to treat the Female Chartists'. This warned that:

> London is threatened with an irruption [sic] of female Chartists, and every man of experience is naturally alarmed, for he knows that the VOX FOEMINAE is the VOX DIABOLI when it is set going . . . we have, however, something to propose that will easily meet the emergency. A heroine who could never run from a man, would fly in dismay before an industrious flea or a burly black beetle. We have only to collect together a good supply of cockroaches, with a fair sprinkling of rats, and

a muster of mice, in order to disperse the largest and most ferocious crowd of females that ever was collected.[52]

But this was good clean fun compared with the words of the Reverend Francis Close of Cheltenham, who accused politically active females of being indelicate, unchristian and vice-ridden. And even this hostility from predominantly conservative middle-class sections of British society must have been easier to accept than the opposition of working women to political activism.[53] It surfaced sometimes during strikes, was noted at Peterloo, and was probably a recurrent theme of Chartism too if the frequent jokes of the male Chartists about women being Tories give any fair indication. Elizabeth Gaskell highlights women's opposition in *Mary Barton*, as does Disraeli in *Sybil*, where the Widow Carey probably spoke for many others of her sex: 'The Widow shook her head. "I don't like these politics", said the good woman, "they baint in a manner of business for our sex." '[54]

Yet for all the expressed opposition and hostility, politics did become the business of women in 1838 – 9, to an extent never previously known and still not accurately measured. During the first great wave of Chartist enthusiasm separate women's organisations sprang up throughout the country in places that had never previously known female associations. The old centres of the north again took the lead, with many anti-Poor Law associations changing their names and broadening their campaigns, but they were joined by new organisations and groups from all corners of the kingdom. The women of Bath, Trowbridge and Bradford-upon-Avon appear to have constituted a very numerous and active West Country force, while those of Brighton mobilised in a more surprising display of political radicalism in the south-east.[55] The organisations and associations took many names. There were Female Charter associations and Women's Charter associations throughout England and Scotland, Female Radical associations, Female Political unions, Female associations, Female Radical Reform associations, Female Patriotic associations, and other groups of a more *ad hoc* nature which were never formally constituted under one of these titles or under some other name. When the Bath Female Radical Association addressed itself in 1840 to 'all the Associations in the Queendom' it doubtless invited the attention of an unnumbered host of variously named bodies which were broadly in sympathy with the Bath Association.[56] Their number still remains elusive. It has been suggested that there were at least eighty separate female unions and associations in being in the period 1837 – 44, and, whilst this is undoubtedly correct, it probably underestimates the degree to which the organisations proliferated.[57] In some places like Stockport there were said to be female radical associations in different parts of the town in June 1839, and in other places, like Manchester and Bradford, the women were sometimes organised on a street basis, such as the 'Female Chartists of Brown Street, East Manchester' in January 1841.[58] How far these neighbourhood groups went towards formalising their structure or whether they existed essentially for collecting purposes or the occasional meeting it is difficult to say, but it seems certain that with some big population centres contributing several organisations, the total number must have been somewhere between a hundred and a thousand, if towards the bottom of this range.

Some of the organisations, like that in Elland, where the formidable trio of Grassby, Hansen and Walker had acquired considerable experience in the anti-Poor Law movement, were fully autonomous from the outset, chairing their own meetings, providing their own speakers, and sometimes, as in the case of Mary Grassby, sending their members far afield to address other groups.[59] Others, such as the Newcastle Female Political Union, were initiated by men and passed subsequently into the control of the women themselves.[60] Sometimes separate men's and women's organisations came together for meetings and demonstrations, and sometimes there was formal unification of the two bodies, which suggests, perhaps misleadingly, that women had by then come to be accepted on equal terms with men. In May 1842, the large Birmingham men's and women's groups were meeting together and being addressed as 'Brother and Sister Chartists', having probably, it has been argued, merged their separate identities two years earlier.[61] This does not indicate an achievement of parity for women within Chartist organisations, for it is notorious that in national councils women did not feature. Some might be chosen as local delegates to regional conferences, as happened to Frances Lewis of Oldham and Elizabeth Ellis and Elizabeth Simpson of Bradford in 1841, but this was probably the limit of their official recognition.[62] William Lovett, despite his declared commitment to women's rights and the abilities of his wife, had no place for her or others in the councils of the London Working Men's Association;

there were no women on the Committee of the National Charter Association, formed in 1840, and women were not normally given the privilege of addressing mixed audiences.

Estimating the number of women actively involved in Chartism presents the same difficulties as estimating the support for any popular movement in the first half of the nineteenth century. The report on the 1848 Chartist petition to Parliament suggested that every 100,000 names contained 8,200 that were women's, but the petitions have been traditionally treated with some scepticism.[63] Even so, the implication that men outnumbered women signatories by more than ten to one is perhaps a little surprising in view of the reported enthusiasm of women in many areas and is probably a reflection of the declining interest that they were showing by 1848. Ten years earlier it was reckoned that 50,000 women signed the national petition within the first fortnight of its existence, and Bronterre O'Brien's expectation was that half a million would eventually sign it, compared with 3 million men.[64] These figures are no more reliable than contemporary estimates of attendance at demonstrations in the open air, though indoor meetings should have been more easy to assess. The claim that Thomas Clutton Salt addressed a gathering of 12,000 women in Birmingham in the spring of 1838 seems rather fanciful, and less reliable than Gammage's belief that there were 1,300 enrolled female Chartists in that place by September 1838, a figure that tallies well with the 1,300 tickets sold for a function which the women were holding.[65] If *Northern Star* reports were true that a room capable of accommodating 800 was crowded to excess for Vincent's address to the Bradford-upon-Avon Female Patriotic Association on 10 June, it is possible that there were 2,000 women present at a market-place meeting two days later.[66] The local association did, after all, boast an enrolled membership of 324 women, compared with the male association's 517 members.[67] At Trowbridge 1,000 radical females were reported to have crowded into a barrack-room meeting.[68]

Sometimes numbers were given with a precision which suggested that a counting exercise had taken place — for example the 320 women who attended a meeting at Thornley, Sunderland, in May 1839, the 366 'gaily dressed' women who attended a radical demonstration at Carlisle in October 1838, or the 160 female radicals of Merthyr Tydfil who attended a tea-party in December 1839 on behalf of the prisoners in Monmouth jail.[69] All these figures are far from conclusive, but they are suggestive. They suggest, for instance, that if Bradford-upon-Avon could mobilise over three hundred, Bradford betwixt Aire and Calder could have done somewhat better and that towns like Manchester, Birmingham and Nottingham would have done considerably better than that. It becomes clear that to talk of tens of thousands of actively organised female Chartists is to express a cautious judgement.

The variety of their activities was also very great. To some extent women, even within their political organisations, continued to perform activities associated with the stereotype, the knitting of scarves, the stitching of caps of liberty, the sewing of banners, for example. Caroline Maria Williams, the London leader, did not despise this kind of contribution and recommended fancy needlework as a way in which more socially conformist women could be of political value.[70] Another such job to be done was the inevitable tea-making, at their own and mixed functions, though tea-parties were rarely undertaken as acts of complete self-indulgence and were more likely to be used as fund-raising operations, morale boosters, or for further political education. More than a hundred women enjoyed an Easter Tuesday tea-party at Rochdale in 1839;[71] a Manchester group of female Chartists, in December 1840, held a tea, followed by an address, and then took part in a social programme of dancing, singing and recitations.[72] In March 1841, women at Bilston, Staffordshire, combined a tea-party with an evening ball. After a tea which was said to have been a 'great credit to the ladies', they moved into the ball, which was interrupted mid-evening for Mr White to address the females on the benefits of good government![73] At Liverpool, in September 1838, a radical dinner in honour of Thomas Attwood, though not attended by that gentleman, was attended by a mixed company, including 180 women, who paid three shillings per head to help boost the Chartist cause.[74]

Fund-raising by direct house-to-house and other collections was one of the main activities of the female Chartist organisations, partly to support the cause in general but also to raise funds on behalf of particular individuals, especially the families of imprisoned Chartists and those who achieved heroic or even martyr status within the movement, John Frost or Samuel Holberry. The women of Nottingham raised money for the families of the radical prisoners in Wales just as the Merthyr women had collected money for the defence of the Newport rioters or rebels, according to judgement.[75] In December 1838 Newcastle women volunteered to help men to collect the 'National Rent', and in March 1839 the women of Bradford took many collections on behalf of the arrested Rev. J. R. Stephens, a Chartist favourite in many northern areas despite his ambiguous relationship with the movement.[76] And when women were not collecting money, and sometimes when they were, they were collecting signatures, as in the case of the women of south Lancashire who embarked on a major petition drive in 1842.[77]

The routine activity was the regular meeting, often a weekly meeting, of the association, but greater publicity was given to the demonstrations, where women were frequently much in evidence and the banners came out on display. The local women were reported to be making great exertions in preparation for the first Kersal Moor demonstration at Manchester in September 1838, for which they were given a special mention in John Fielden's speech.[78] At the second Kersal Moor demonstration of May 1839, women were even more prominent in the account given by the *Manchester Guardian*.[79] They attended in force the great West Riding demonstration at Peep Green, Hartshead, in October 1838, and in 1839 displayed their banners at Barnsley, Bradford, Macclesfield, Colne, Nottingham, Aberdeen and many other places.[80] The banners emphasised female political involvement through pictorial representation of radical women bearing the cap of liberty and the Charter, as at Macclesfield, in August, or declaring their aims and grievances in the language of religion.[81] In October 1838 the women of Marsden attended a demonstration at Colne demanding political freedom 'most vociferously' and carrying banners which displayed the following messages;

Every man hath a right to one vote in the choice of his representatives; and it belongs to him in the right of his existence, and his person is his title deed.

Whoso stoppeth his ears at the cry of the poor he also shall cry for himself, but shall not be heard. Prov. xxi, 13.

No imprisonment for poverty where caused by taxation.[82]

Much of this time it is difficult to know how strong the female presence at a meeting or demonstration was because of the disparaging nature of the comments being passed and because the women were referred to incidentally or for purposes of insult. The Peep Green demonstration of October 1838 was said to have been less impressive than its organisers intended because 'one third consisted of women and children', and a Bradford meeting in the same month was said to have had 800 people present 'exclusive of three or four carts full of women', as though they were a separate category of beings.[83] The principal attenders at a Bolton demonstration in the November were said to be 'young women and a number of Irishmen', another unflattering association, whilst the Macclesfield demonstration of August 1839 was said to be 'pathetically small' even allowing for the women and boys present, who evidently did not really count.[84] A radical demonstration at Oldham in November 1838 allegedly attracted crowds of boys and young women because of the noise and the bright lights, as though the political purpose would have had no appeal, and the women who attended demonstrations in Manchester and Salford in July 1839 were identified by their shouting and generally noisy conduct.[85] Such reporting of events certainly detracts from the view of serious-minded women attending political meetings and demonstrations from serious intent.

There could be no detracting from the impressive gathering of members of the Manchester Female Political Union on Christmas Day 1840, when 1,000 of them, many wearing garlands and wreaths of evergreen, demonstrated on behalf of recently liberated patriots. They were attended by a brass band, and the speaker, Mr Doyle, addressed the assembled throng as 'Ladies and Brother Radicals of Manchester'.[86] On New Year's Day, 1841, there was a London demonstration involving a procession in which many allegedly 'thinly clad females' took part; the *Weekly Chronicle*, which reported this event in these terms, was invited to say whether this reporting was a piece of provocative mischief-making or indeed a genuine indication of the fact that poor women were insufficiently protected from the chilling cold in the capital of the world's richest country.[87] Other women made their mark in other ways: those who organised a Female Democratic Festival at Newcastle in June 1839; the Bath females who tried to organise a demonstration in the highest of places by having the women of the Welsh convicts appear personally before the Queen; the Bath females again who provided six of their number to carry the coffin of a departed colleague at a funeral in September 1842; or the women who went out to welcome O'Connor during his Midlands pilgrimage of May

1842 through Staffordshire and Derbyshire:[88]

> When we arrived at Lane End [wrote O'Connor] I thought that all the world had come there. The town was literally full. Though the rain fell in torrents, every window and house top was crowded. The poor fellows sent a carriage and four for me, and in front was a splendid military band, and in advance the female Chartists, about 300 — God bless them — with their band, each woman bearing a wand. They intended to have marched me thus about eleven miles, but cut it down to seven in consequence of the rain.

Less peaceful were the activities of the female Chartists that ended up in a riot, a nice reversion to traditional violence and direct action even within the context of this sophisticated political movement. There were riots at Llandidloes in May 1839 when males were allegedly incited by female reformers who carried stones for them, another auxiliary role and one of the rare occasions on which female Chartists were arrested.[89] And in June 1838 five men and two women were responsible for attacking the barracks at Trowbridge and firing at a policeman.[90] At Rochdale, in August, a crowd of thousands contained a large contingent of women, said to be 'ten times more furious than the men'; one woman, with a child of a few months in her arms, was reported to have been 'exceedingly busy exciting the multitude to attack the soldiers'.[91] Women were very prominent in disturbances in Middleton and Manchester at the same time, and one woman, Mary Holmes, was charged with throwing stones at the police. Because she was given a good character and supported herself and a lame husband by taking in washing she was dismissed, but required to keep the peace for one month.[92] In his fictionalised account of the Plug Plot riots in *Sybil*, Disraeli stressed the working women's enthusiastic involvement in torchlight mass meetings and riots, and he had women present in the throng from Wodgate who pulled the plugs at Trafford's Mill during the National Holiday. A young worker, disillusioned with male apathy, noted the contrasting female enthusiasm. 'The gals is the only thing what has any spirit left. Julia told me just now she would go to the cannon's mouth for the Five Points any summer day.'[93]

This willingness to indulge in rhetoric far beyond anything actually envisaged, and certainly well beyond anything actually undertaken, was a characteristic of women's Chartism just as it was of men's. There were many fiery declarations and promises made on behalf of the glorious cause and many expressions of a willingness to risk life itself for the preservation of freedom. When the women of Bradford took collections for J. R. Stephens in March 1839 they expressed a willingness to go and release him themselves if the need arose:

> should they get up a packed jury of cotton lords, to pronounce a verdict of guilty against him, and they should imprison, transport, or bring him to the scaffold, we will go . . . to release him from the hands of our oppressors; and should we die in the struggle, we shall account our deaths a thousand times better, a thousand times happier, than that of dying in a Whig Bastile [sic].[94]

Similarly, women of Stalybridge expressed a determination to oppose the New Poor Law to the death and to resist the introduction of a rural police, another issue that came to be caught up in Chartism.[95] Elizabeth Mallett, of Sunderland, informed her co-Chartists that she had learned what pistols were made for; let God help tyranny on the banks of the Wear and Tyne; the time had come for action; let the women of the Tyne stand forward.[96] In similar vein Mrs Gascoigne of Darlington boasted that she had pulled a trigger before, and would, presumably, be willing to do it again.[97]

Such threatening language was hardly mainstream women's Chartism, and it is interesting to observe that some women's leaders noted the disparity between words and action. Caroline Maria Williams, for example, warned against the possibility that women might make themselves ridiculous:

> do not let them point at us the finger of scorn and say, 'Look at those poor wretches; what a fuss they make; they talk, talk, and that is all they can do; they say but do not.' No, my friends, but let us by God's help resolve that from this moment our apathy shall cease . . . we will arouse ourselves from our lethargy, and with untiring zeal begin not only to talk, but to work out our political salvation.[99]

It was easier said than done. Miss Groves, the Chairwoman of the

Birmingham Female Political Union, echoed this concern in a bitter address, delivered in 1839, which censured the Birmingham women's empty resolutions: 'She remembered, upon one occasion, Collins prophecying [sic] that he should be imprisoned, and that the women then rose in a body and exclaimed — "then we will fetch you out". Where were those women now?'[99] The problem of empty words did not pass unnoticed, though Miss Groves in particular went on to suggest only forms of action which would be tackled successfully by even the most timid of women, such as the collecting of funds to support the families of political prisoners.

Another technique that required no great personal courage, though it might involve a breach in customary routines and some financial self-sacrifice, was that of selective shopping or exclusive dealing. One thing women could do, as an extension of their housekeeping duties, was to discriminate against those merchants or shopkeepers who were unwilling to declare themselves in support of the Chartist cause and to reward those who did. The practice is known to have been implemented in a great many places, including Bradford, Leeds, Stockport, Carlisle, Darlington, Bristol and other areas of strength, and to have persisted throughout at least a decade of Chartism, though with what degree of intensity or success it is impossible to say. In July 1839 Mrs Tanfield of Darlington resolved, on behalf of her members, 'to support those shop-keepers who support the rights of industry', a somewhat obscure declaration and less explicit than Mrs McIlcoy's resolution, on behalf of the Carlisle Female Radical Association, in December 1838, to 'spend our earnings with none but those who are willing to be co-workers with us in the great work of national redemption, and are willing to contribute their mite towards the support of the same'.[100] There were reports in August of pressure being put upon Bradford shopkeepers to subscribe to Chartist funds, on pain of loss of trade, and in October the women of Leeds pledged themselves 'to deal with none who are against the sacred cause'.[101] Not surprisingly, the practice of opening Chartist co-operative stores was sometimes preferred as an alternative technique. In August 1840, for instance, the Calton Female Universal Suffrage Association held a crowded meeting, attended by a number of men, who appear to have taken responsibility for drawing up 'the articles of the Chartist Provision Store'; shares were five shillings each and were rapidly being acquired. 'After the business, the meeting were entertained by several comic songs from Messrs. Drummond,

Hamilton, etc.'; and so light relief was brought to a serious meeting.[102]

But for all their efforts, women failed to achieve the vote for working-class men, which was their avowed purpose, though it must be asked if this was their only purpose and if they remained content to fulfil this auxiliary role without any expressed wish for political rights for themselves. Critics of Chartism were not lacking to point out that the campaign for universal suffrage, whether waged by men or by women, was a calculated hypocrisy as long as universal meant manhood suffrage. This did not mean that the *Leeds Mercury* or the *Manchester Guardian*, for example, wished to advocate votes for women, only that they were finding one more reason for disagreeing with Chartism. Yet despite this hypocrisy or lack of logic, universal suffrage continued to mean manhood suffrage to most Chartists, and the history of Chartism contained no public rallies or meetings specifically for the purpose of achieving women's rights. These constituted only a minor theme of Chartism, even among Chartist women, though the latter were not so impervious to the implications of their campaign for political democracy to remain unaware of the inferences that their more advanced leaders were beginning to draw. The increased political activity of women during Chartism inevitably prompted the re-opening of the wider debate on the role and rights of women within society, conducted in part within middle-class periodicals like the *Edinburgh Review* and the *Quarterly Review*, but also given wide coverage in the Chartist press, the *Northern Star* and the *English Chartist Circular*.

In 1841 there appeared both a new work on *The Rights of Women*, by R. J. Richardson, and a timely reprint of Mary Wollstonecraft's classic on the same subject, excerpts from which appeared regularly in those sections of the press which were sympathetic to the promotion of the discussion. Such writings and such discussions ensured that Chartist women, who expended so much of their time and energies on rationalising their involvement, as women, in politics, should also come to consider that what they did they did by right, and that furthermore they were entitled to do other things too. Sophia of Birmingham sought to overcome male prejudices against women's political involvement and equal rights to enjoy such involvement, but it was Susannah Inge, the powerful leader of the City of London Female Charter Association, who railed against existing women's slavery:

Rouse yourselves to a sense of your merits. Assist those men who will, nay, who do, place women in an equality with themselves in gaining their rights, and yours will be gained also . . . Do not say you have no business with politics, and that you leave such things for your husbands, fathers and brothers. You have an interest in politics, a deeper interest than you are aware of.[103]

This was consistent with the declaration of the female radicals of Keighley in October 1839 to the females of the United Kingdom, when they urged: 'If you, then, are wishful to be free, stand up with a bold front, like women determined to shake off the bonds of despotism, and join with us in demanding our just rights.'[104] Women's rights were an issue in the West Riding of Yorkshire as well as in the metropolis, and not only in these places. It was the Gorbals Female Universal Suffrage Association which declared in December 1839 that women were not always the helpmates of man, as the Creator intended; rather were they beasts of burden.[105] The East London Female Chartist Association announced portentously that 'Woman has hitherto been deemed and treated as man's inferior. Let us the women endeavour to remove this reproach.' They resolved to set an example, which men would surely follow, albeit, on this occasion, the example of temperance![106] Other women demonstrated their independence in other ways. In March 1841 a woman, attempting to have her child christened James Feargus O'Connor King, was asked by the registrar if her husband was a Chartist. She professed ignorance on this matter, conveying only the knowledge that his wife was.[107]

Although it would be correct to say that 'votes for women' was not a major issue during Chartism, it is not correct to say that the issue of women's suffrage was not raised until after 1848, and then for the first time by Helen Macfarlane, the translator of the *Communist Manifesto*.[108] Well before then an increasing number of male Chartist leaders had begun to advocate women's right to vote as part of universal suffrage. Lovett, having failed to embody the principle within the original Charter, proposed the eventually accepted inclusion of women within the National Charter Association on the grounds that they were equally liable to punishment under the law and ought therefore to have an equal say in the determination of the law; that females contributed to taxation and that there should be no taxation without representation; women shared in their husbands' political affairs and so should share in their rights.[109] In April 1841 John Watkins of London argued that 'women ought to be allowed to vote', but he limited women to maids and widows on the grounds that wives were really as one with their husbands. His support for women's franchise he based on the not very encouraging reasoning that, while women might not do any better than their men, they could scarcely make matters worse.[110]

Such limitations and such arguments are typical of the prejudices, hesitations and ambiguities that pervade the attitudes of even those male Chartists who appeared to champion the women's cause. Dorothy Thompson notes, for instance, that even R. J. Richardson, in his book on *The Rights of Women*, thought that only spinsters and widows should be enfranchised since the political rights of the two sexes became merged on marriage. She also identifies the fear of some male Chartists that advocacy of the women's cause was likely to delay the achievement of their own.[111] The championship of such men as Julian Harney, who believed that women should participate as fully as men in society, or Bronterre O'Brien, who believed that women had the same inherent rights as men and the same motives for concerning themselves in politics as men had, still left women without a substantial base of clear, unequivocal support for their own political enfranchisement.[112]

Nor, of course, were advocates of women's rights anything more than a minority within the ranks of the female activists themselves. The London Female Democratic Association declared in 1839: 'we assert in accordance with the rights of all . . . our right, as free women (or women determined to be free) to rule ourselves,' but few were openly interested in pursuing their right at this stage.[113] One who was, the anonymous authoress of a letter to the *Northern Star* in June 1838, signed herself 'A Real Democrat'. Although 'a plain working woman — a weaver of Glasgow', who had herself been denied opportunities of education, she declared, quite unambiguously, 'It is the right of every woman to have a vote in the legislation of her country,' a position that not even the Suffragettes of later days were to uphold in such clear terms.[114] But despite a few individual statements of this kind, the overall demand was so slight that it prompted George Holyoake to suppose that women's failure to request political rights must indicate the absence of any wish to possess them. More likely, as R. S. Neale explains, the traditional subservience and dependence of their sex, allied to the traditional deference of their class, were too great to be readily overcome.[115]

It is interesting to observe that the women who worked for the Anti-Corn Law League during the middle Chartist period were treated to similar sorts of comments from the press and male opponents as the female Chartists, despite the differences in social background. Hostility was evidently based on sex rather than class. Middle-class women were slower to enter the political arena in support of their cause than were the working-class ones, perhaps because they were even more constrained by conventional notions on what was acceptable female behaviour, but in the early 1840s the wives of prominent League men and other women began to undertake the same sort of tasks for the League that Chartist women had been performing: holding meetings, organising tea parties, conducting appeals, being responsible for house-to-house collections of money and signatures, and distributing circulars. In similar fashion they supported their husbands and they paid similar tributes to their male leaders when the individuals had the necessary charisma to command their affection; in July 1845, for instance, May and Roba Brady of Leavy Grove presented Cobden with a pair of slippers as a token of their admiration.[116] Unlike the female Chartists, the Leaguers appear to have formed no separate female anti-Corn Law societies. Characteristic was the Manchester Ladies' Committee, with some 200 members, which, in a rare act of independence, itself organised a bazaar.[117] On the whole they acted a subservient role and voiced no aspirations on behalf of women. It was significant that they were inclined to portray their work as charity, which fitted well into the conventional mould.

Yet this did not protect them from all abuse. J. W. Croker, in the *Quarterly Review*, affected to see the female Leaguers as violent political partisans, offensive to good taste and destructive of the best feminine virtues; the Manchester bazaar was merely camouflage for more sinister purposes, for 'It has been a frequent device of revolutionary agitators to bring women forward as a screen and safeguard to their own operations.'[118] A more common response was that produced by the Tory *Leeds Intelligencer*:

We are truly sorry to see females, many of whom move in a respectable sphere of life, forgetful that home is their proper sphere of actions, and that domestic management is their paramount duty, rambling about from house to house collecting signatures to a petition . . . Where in the name of wonder will this humbugging sort of petticoat policy end! It is lamentable to behold females making themselves not merely ridiculous, but absolutely contemptible.[119]

The paper was not unhappy to report that women collectors had been urged to go home and mend their stocking heels, though it was less happy, on a later occasion, to report that 'many rebuffs do they meet with, and such as in some instances no modest woman ought to put herself in the way of incurring'.[120]

But not even the appearance of middle-class women in the political arena was sufficient to sustain the momentum of women's involvement. Even in the early 1840s accounts of women's meetings and other activities began to decline in number in these columns that had reported them so enthusiastically during the period 1838 – 40. There are several possible explanations of this. One is that women's activities, which had once been so novel and therefore so newsworthy, lost a lot of their appeal as they became more commonplace. Another is that, in an increasingly faction-ridden and divided movement, women might have tried to make their contribution to unity by amalgamating their activities and organisations with those of the men, to whom they became more acceptable as near-equal partners in a common campaign. Some independent women's organisations remained, such as the Female National Charter Association of Bradford, which proudly displayed its banners at Skircoat Moor in April 1848, but women were now less likely to receive a separate mention as forming a prominent part of a demonstration or a crowd at a meeting.[121] According to *Punch*, London was 'threatened with an irruption of female Chartists in 1848', but satirical copy rather than political fear was the inspiration of the comment.[122] Even as late as 1851 new organisations were still being formed, such as the Sheffield Female Political Association, and it would clearly be rash to suggest that women's activities came to an end.[123]

None the less it is difficult to resist Dorothy Thompson's conclusion that women had largely disappeared from working-class politics before the middle of the century, that the new awareness and self-confidence discovered in the Chartist period were only temporary gains, to be lost as women reverted to an acceptance of the social stereotype, re-imposed with perhaps greater force in the mid-Victorian period than before.[124] In part the decline in the political activities of working-class women paralleled the decline of those of the working classes as a whole, and for similar reasons: Chartism, the 'bread and butter' question, declined in appeal as more prosperous times were reached, substitutes such as co-operative shopping appeared, Poor Law administration became more 'humanised', and so on. In easier times the 'direct challenge of mass politics' was left behind, workers' protest became 'institutionalised' and softened through trade unionism, and the women, like the great mass of unskilled workers, found that they had been abandoned and forgotten. At a time when, it has been argued, women had been fully integrated into factory employment and accordingly into working-class politics, married women were increasingly choosing to stay at home on the birth of their children, thereby encouraging the re-imposition of the stereotype concept and perhaps weakening the impetus towards political involvement. And if the men were being diverted from political agitation to the accumulation of accounts in savings banks, so too were some women diverted from politics to temperance, a cause more fitting the conventional view of a woman's role.[125]

By the mid-century both working- and middle-class women had experienced considerable involvement in political protest of different kinds; whether they had played a vital and influential role in the history of their respective movements is more difficult to say, though it is certainly clear that the extent of women's involvement in Chartism has traditionally been much underestimated, where not completely ignored. The intent of the female Chartists was more important than their achievement. The same is true of that small number of women Chartists who launched the campaign for women's rights within the context of the working-class political movement.

POSTSCRIPT: REBECCA AND HER SISTERS

The study of women's part in social and political protest is still very much in its early stages, and a great deal of work remains to be done on both the factual and interpretative sides of the subject. One subject for possible investigation is that of the activities of those men, by no means rare, who put on women's clothes in preparation for their protest operations. This phenomenon appears to suggest that men consciously and deliberately chose women as symbols of what they were doing and attempting to achieve, and that they were thereby according women a particular role of importance within social protest. Before the idea of organising to acquire equal rights for their sex had crossed the minds of more than a tiny number of women, some of their men were projecting themselves as women in order, apparently, to express themselves more effectively. This was a persistently recurring theme of social protest, that men dressed themselves in female attire, and quasi-women appeared in Luddism, the Swing riots, Scotch Cattle, the Rebecca riots and the Scottish Clearance riots. The history and full extent of this phenomenon are not known, but it is a sufficiently common theme of the early nineteenth century to warrant investigation for the light that it might throw on the supposed role of real women in social protest as well as the pretending men. In the period before organised feminism, women appear to have played a distinctive active role in popular protest, both in their own right as women and as female symbols for male protest in those matters where women were themselves most prominent.

The machine breaking or Luddism of the years 1811 – 16, widespread throughout the east Midlands and west Yorkshire and spilling over into south Lancashire, provides no publicised examples of men dressing up as women to carry out their industrial protest, for blackened faces were their usual disguise. In fact, only in the collective rioting of Lancashire Luddism did women feature at all. But this did not prevent a contemporary cartoonist from portraying Ned Ludd, the mythical leader of machine breakers, disguised as a woman, which has been explained by the suggestion that this was intended to be disparaging, condemning the Luddite leader for obscuring his identity and not appearing out in the open.[1]

The interpretation is probably a mistaken one, for General Ludd was no more a single identity than Captain Swing or Rebecca, and there were few who believed in a single leader of a national movement. It is more likely that the cartoonist was allowing protest to assume a female form, as it frequently did, and that he was placing Luddism within accepted and recognised traditions. During 1812, and particularly in April, not only were women in frequent action in their most familiar context, that of food rioting, but men were also in action, dressed as women. Two principal leaders of the Stockport crowds were men dressed in women's clothes who described themselves as 'General Ludd's wives', in contrast with the 'Lady Ludd' who led the crowds in Nottingham and Leeds, for this part was played by a woman. On 14 April, the large Stockport crowds, led by men in women's clothing, stoned the home of Mr Goodair, an owner of steam looms, at Edgeley, and later returned with the aid of reinforcements to fire his house.[2]

Transvestism is not a strong theme in Luddism, but it is present. The same can be said of its incidence in the Swing riots. As with Luddism, the general disguise for bands of agricultural machine breakers and arsonists was blackened faces, where disguise was thought necessary, and contemporary accounts reveal only one instance where Swing and his followers were disguised as women. In November 1830 six threshing machines were broken at St Nicholas, Monckton, and Minster in Kent, and amongst the rioting crowd 'some of the men were disguised in female attire'.[3] No particular reason for this form of disguise is discernible, and this occasion was an exception to the normal Swing pattern of protest.

The theme is at its strongest in Wales, reaching a peak during the Rebecca riots, 1838 – 43, but present in earlier protest movements, such as that which greeted the enclosing Commissioners and progressive landowners of Cardiganshire in the late eighteenth and early nineteenth centuries, when they infringed and eliminated what were thought to be popular, traditional rights, such as the right to cut turf. On such occasions, it has been said, the people's 'Turf Act' replaced the official Enclosure Acts, and offenders against the people's code could expect to receive threatening letters and 'visits by mobs disguised as women'.[4] One such recipient was Augustus Brackenbury, who made a sworn statement before JPs in Cardiganshire in July 1820 to the effect that he had been threatened ever since buying waste or common land in the area. He had been ordered to demolish fences and other erections but had chosen to go ahead with building his house and occupying it. This had caused him to be confronted by 'assemblages with firearms'. On one particular occasion a crowd set fire to and destroyed his house, several of the men having covered their faces with handkerchiefs for disguise, 'and he verily believes that others of the Men were dressed in women's clothes'.[5] This has been interpreted as 'an extension of ordinary rural revelry such as the mock trial'.[6]

The same has been said of the protest movement of Scotch Cattle, which employed many forms of violence to demonstrate against unemployment throughout the mining districts in the period 1820 – 35. The leaders were disguised by masks and cattle-skins, but their followers blackened their faces and wore female clothing, a curiously excessive precaution if disguise were the only purpose of their elaborate preparations, which seems unlikely. Their leader was 'Lolly', the 'Rebecca' of the coalfields, head of a family of 900 faithful children, and his followers' disguises were adaptations of the old mock-trial procedures: sometimes they wore women's clothes, sometimes reversed jackets or 'turncoats'. Animal skins, women's dresses or turncoats were accepted symbols for legitimate expression of rural solidarity, of the community in pursuit of justice, just as men in women's clothes might lead village revelry on other occasions.[7] This may help to explain the appearance of the quasi-women in Welsh protest, but it is not sufficient to explain their appearance in other areas within and beyond the Celtic fringes; nor is it an explanation of 'first causes', for it leaves unanswered the question of how women's clothes came to be a token of community justice.

The most complete identification of a British social protest movement with women, and the one containing most examples of transvestism, was that of the Rebecca riots, a series of attacks on toll-gates and other targets in west Wales during the years 1838 – 43. The mythical leader of the protestors was Rebecca, and so complete was the development of the myth that the historian of the movement has been content to personify protest and speak consistently of the movement as if it were a woman.[8] Rebecca's followers were her sons and daughters, and the success of her operations so established her within folk tradition that many today are still proud to be considered Rebecca's children.

General rural distress, and specific grievances about the New Poor Law, tithes and especially the toll-gates throughout Carmarthenshire, Pembrokeshire and Cardiganshire created a series of issues, fundamentally economic, of a kind that tradition-ally engaged women's sympathies, though the response to these came less from women than from men who identified themselves with a leader called Rebecca. In January 1839 the first band of men dressed in women's clothing destroyed two gates on the Carmarthen/Pembrokeshire borders.[9] On 17 July occurred a more significant incident, when a crowd of men assembled at Efailwen, with blackened faces and wearing women's clothes. Their leader was addressed as 'Becca' because, it was said, he had had difficulty in finding clothes to fit him and needed to borrow from 'Big Rebecca' in a neighbouring parish.[10] Although this particular individual played no part in the subsequent riots the name stuck, and every group leader became another Rebecca just as every leader of a Luddite band had been General Ludd for the night in 1811 – 12. The story is plausible enough. What it fails totally to explain is why the individual concerned, one Thomas Rees, had felt it necessary to attire himself in women's clothes in the first place. Yet the wearing of women's clothing was to continue to be a characteristic feature of the movement. On 12 December 1842 between 70 and 100 men in women's clothes destroyed all the toll-gates of St Clears at midnight, and in June 1842 about 150 men visited Llanfihangel-ar-arth, all of whom wore women's clothes, some with masks and some with painted faces.[11] In June 1843 rioters at the Pen-y-garn gate near Newcastle Emlyn and outside Carmarthen town wore turbans or women's caps.[12] By contrast, a crowd that entered Carmarthen, estimated at 300 on horseback and 2,000 on foot, was led by a single symbolic Rebecca, 'disguised with a woman's curls', which were probably a horsehair wig, and wearing a woman's dress.[13] Occasionally the mood was light-hearted, to the point of frivolity. In July 1843 the Rebecca who led an attack on the Penrallt gate near Llanelbyther was 'dressed gaily in female attire and sported a parasol'.[14]

It is ironic that while the Rebecca rioters dressed as women and had a symbolically female leader, their attitude towards women rioters was one of exclusion. A secret meeting of Rebeccaites at Cwm Ivor in July 1843 confirmed this faith in symbolic female leadership in the resolution that: 'If any man rents his neighbour's farm treacherously, we must acquaint the lady [Rebecca], and endeavour to encourage her exertions wherever she wishes for us to execute our phenomena and combat.' However, a further resolu-tion prohibited the entry of youths under the age of eighteen, and females 'except Rebecca and Miss Cromwell', the second person presumably being the daughter of the Great Protector, and both exclusively male roles.[15]

This exclusion of women is balanced by an apparent concern displayed by Rebecca for rectifying wrongs suffered by women in their relationships with men, for she soon began to broaden her activities beyond the issue of toll gates; in her concern that illegitimate children should be brought to the attention of their fathers; her threats to young men who were hesitating over marriage to girls they had compromised; her visits to husbands who were accused of beating their wives; her attempts at reconciliation within troubled marriages.[16] All these activities were undertaken by Rebecca in her alternative role as guardian of public morality, rather than as the upholder of women's rights, but she appears to have attributed rights to at least the women she rescued.

It is interesting, in view of the apparent wish to exclude women from protest, that at the largest mass Rebecca riot, the destruction of the Carmarthen workhouse in June 1843, not only was Miss Rebecca in attendance but also a large number of women amongst the crowd estimated at between 10,000 and 12,000. This was the occasion when Frances Evans danced on the hall table and led the mob up the workhouse stairs.[17]

The main contribution of women, however, apart from lending their clothes, seems to have been that of supplying a female symbol for the leadership and organisation of the Welsh riots; for all threatening letters were signed by Rebecca and all activities were carried out in her name, which was sometimes cited as Rebecca Dogood.[18] Even the dating of a series of resolutions appeared as 'Thursday, the 20th day of May in the first year of Rebecca's exploits, A.D. 1843', though this was not in fact the first year of her exploits.[19] Despite the many attempts to identify a male as the single leader of the movement, no one person was found for the role, and it must be concluded that there was no clear leadership, no single Rebecca, just as there had been no Ned Ludd or Captain Swing, and no mastermind, as the authorities for a long time believed. Rebecca's importance lay in her role as a symbolic female figurehead which provided the rallying point for diverse social protest.

Perhaps the best clue to her origins is to be found in a *Times* report from the scene of the riots: 'The lower orders in Wales have a considerable degree of religious fanaticism about them, are most of them Dissenters, and are in the constant habit of quoting scripture for everything which they advance.'[20]

The most logical explanation of Rebecca seems to be that of her scriptural origins, for Genesis, Chapter 24, verse 60 relates: 'And they blessed Rebeckah and said unto her "Thou art our sister, be thou the mother of thousands of millions, and let thy seed possess the gate of those which hate thee".'

The steadfast mother of the Old Testament re-emerged in west Wales in the early nineteenth century with an apparently appropriate scriptural reference to toll-gates and a justification for their destruction. This seems entirely comprehensible in a land where the Rev. Eleazer Evans, of the established Church, received a threatening letter demanding the return of tithes paid to the 'National Whore'; otherwise his house would be destroyed just as Gideon threw down the altar of Baal.[21] Although the Wesleyan Methodists stood apart from their fellow Nonconformists, as they frequently did, most preachers of the dissenting communities, Baptists and Independants of various kinds, condoned Rebecca's actions and drew inspiration from the Genesis text. Religion was an active force supporting social protest in Wales, unlike in the Scottish Highlands, where local ministers joined with the evicting landlords and their agents to try to instil a spirit of fatalistic acceptance amongst crofters. The use of a female Biblical character, a woman of great strength, as a symbolic leader, must go some way to explaining why Welsh farmers should disguise themselves as women to achieve a closer identification with their female figurehead while performing her task of social redress.

Of different intent were the crofters who donned women's clothes in the Clearance riots; in this area too it has been recently observed that 'the transvestite element — of men dressing as women — was another recurrent feature of Highland disturbances.'[22] Several incidents have been cited of 'men in women's clothes'; in the Culrain riots of 1820 it was reported that officials were 'obliged to retire and leave the field to these amazons, some of whom were supposed to be gentlemen in female attire', though at least one report, in *The Black Dwarf*, failed to detect the presence of this group of men.[23] Later at Grinds, near Unapool, a sheriff's party attempted to serve a removal notice and 'a great number of women (or I should rather imagine men in female attire) attacked the party and stripped the clothes off them and sent them home stark naked and tore all their papers.'[24] The comment of a Sunderland agent in 1821 that 'the opinion of the people here is that a woman can do anything with impunity' throws some light on why men chose to masquerade as women, and other evidence suggests that the authorities were inclined to look for male offenders rather than female ones.[25]

Not all cases of men in women's clothing relate to the Highlands, for an incident is reported in July 1792 of the destruction of toll-bars near Greenlaw. A farm labourer who had declined to participate in this activity testified that he had been eating his supper when he had been disturbed by a body of about fifteen men, 'some in women's clothes', who had vainly tried to force him to join them.[26] Nor were all cases confined to popular protest that arose from severe economic grievances, though they seem to predominate, for the *Leeds Mercury* reported an interesting case that arose during the political demonstrations in the town during the 'May Days' of 1832, when the reform crisis was at its height. In one of the many protests organised against the Duke of Wellington, 'at the head of one of the processions was a man borne on the shoulders of others, ludicrously attired in women's clothes with a black veil over his face'.[27] Doubtless the black veil had a particular symbolic importance at a time when the fate of the Reform Bill was in the balance and revolution was being widely threatened.

The reasons behind transvestism in social protest are not easy to elucidate. The contemporary term most commonly used to describe the borrowed attire was 'disguise', and David Williams, in his authoritative history of the Rebecca riots, does not go beyond this. Although he notes that there were widespread riots in the West Country in 1749, when some of the rioters were disguised in women's clothes and offers disguise as an implied explanation of the nineteenth-century phenomenon, he has little to say on this subject.[28] And this explanation is undermined by his own account of inadequate concealment of identity, particularly the story of the dressed-up man who winked at a boy who recognised him behind what was evidently a transparent enough disguise of women's clothing and outrageously long horsehair ringlets.[29] It appears that female clothing as used by General Ludd's wives, Swing rioters and Rebeccaites was never intended as a complete disguise, as the rioting labourers were all locally well known, although their identities were kept secret from the authorities in a display of powerful community solidarity. In fact, female clothing tended to attract attention to rather than distract it from the activities of the protestors, and this could have been one of its purposes when *coups* were carried out with light-hearted panache. Female clothing was therefore more important as symbolism in economic protest than as any sort of effective disguise.

A possible motivation for female attire in these working-class protests lies in the type of female apparel worn. The Rebecca rioters' horsehair ringlets, parasols and fashionable dresses were all more prevalent among upper-class women than the rioters' working-class womenfolk. It is possible that through the wearing of such garments the Rebeccaites and Luddites were attacking the women who most represented their opponents, the leisured upper-class landowners and financiers, and the gentry-dominated established Church. Contemporary radical journals repeatedly censured the idle, upper-class women's loose morals and artificial fashions, such as hair falling in ringlets over the forehead or down the neck.[30] Sentiments such as this quite possibly influenced the wearing of such attire in a satirical attack by working-class protestors. Alternatively it could be that, as in modern 'drag' performances, the most grotesque exaggeration of female attire and mannerisms achieved the most widespread popular response.

The suggestion that these working-class male rioters donned female attire because of any pleasure derived from such deviant practices has very little rational support. Likewise, accusations of effeminacy would be difficult to justify, first among such a large, diverse group of protestors, and secondly in a rural labouring environment where any apparent lack of masculinity would have been treated with derision by other men. Also, the activities in which these quasi-women engaged were often extremely hazardous, required considerable physical strength, especially with the added hindrance of unaccustomed long skirts, and could have had disastrous consequences for the participants if detected and brought to trial. Eccentricity is another possible explanation that must be rejected, for contemporary witnesses did not comment on the protestors' sanity, nor suggest anything unusual in such behaviour; even official reports emphasised the outrageous criminal nature of such protest, never questioning the outrageous garb in which it was performed.

It is equally inconclusive to attribute the wearing of female attire to an expectation of lighter treatment before the law. As has been revealed, both women and quasi-women were subjected to severe penalties for illegal protest. Women's clothes certainly did not reduce the great risk attached to active protest, and only in the Highland disturbances does it seem likely that men's dress was supposed to give them advantage. Female disguises were never meant to turn riot into masquerade, rather to provide a symbolic rationale for male involvement in a traditionally female protest area.

The fact that economic protest of the type engaged in by the Luddite and Rebeccaite 'women' was considered a female domain holds the key to the most likely explanation of transvestism in popular riots. Although sometimes requiring male brute strength, as in the destruction of toll-gates or workhouses, such acts were seen to acquire a measure of legitimacy when performed by quasi-women that was denied them if undisguised men were the perpetrators. Social protest, when economic and domestic issues were at stake, was evidently seen as women's work; women's participation in food riots was a well established tradition. As the guardians of the home and family, and of the standards of living necessary to preserve these institutions, women were viewed as the embodiment of justice, humanity and a traditional culture, at risk when social protest occurred. Where women were themselves unable to uphold rights and standards because they lacked the physical strength or stamina for nocturnal destruction, the next best thing to a woman was a man in women's clothing.

NOTES

Chapter 1

1. G. F. E. Rudé, *Protest and Punishment* (Oxford, 1978), pp. 4, 5, 10, 147.
2. G. F. E. Rudé, *The Crowd in History: a Study of Popular Disturbances in France and England, 1730 – 1848* (New York, 1964), p. 205.
3. E. P. Thompson, *The Making of the English Working Class* (London, 1968 edn), p. 13; Iain McCalman, 'Females, Feminism and Free Love in an Early Nineteenth Century Radical Movement', *Labour History*, no. 38 (1980).
4. E. P. Thompson, 'The Moral Economy of the English Crowd in the Eighteenth Century', *Past and Present*, no. 50 (February 1971).
5. E.g. Kenneth J. Logue, *Popular Disturbances in Scotland, 1780 – 1815* (Edinburgh, 1979), p. 199.
6. Rudé, *Protest and Punishment*, Ch. 4.
7. D. J. V. Jones, *Before Rebecca; Popular Protests in Wales, 1793 – 1835* (London, 1973), Ch. 1.
8. Sheila Rowbotham, *Hidden from History* (London, 1973), p. 34.
9. E.g. Janet Vaux, 'Women Workers and Trade Unions in Nineteenth Century Britain', *Hecate*, vol. 4 (1978).
10. R. S. Neale, *Class and Ideology in the Nineteenth Century* (London and Boston, 1972), p. 151.
11. John Foster, *Class Struggle and the Industrial Revolution* (London, 1974), p. 253.
12. Jane Humphries, 'The Working Class Family, Women's Liberation, and Class Struggle: the Case of Nineteenth Century British History', *Review of Radical Political Economics*, vol. 9, no. 3 (1977).
13. E.g. *Manchester Guardian*, 29 September 1838.
14. *Leeds Intelligencer*, 16 April 1842.
15. E. J. Hobsbawm and G. F. E. Rudé, *Captain Swing* (London, 1969), p. 246.
16. Sheila Lewenhak, *Women and Trade Unions* (London, 1977), p. 13.
17. *Northern Star*, 17 March 1838.
18. Logue, *Popular Disturbances*, p. 191.
19. *Leeds Mercury*, 26 May 1838.
20. *Leeds Mercury*, 13 June 1812.
21. *Leeds Mercury*, 25 January 1812.
22. *Manchester Chronicle*, 10 July 1819.
23. *Leeds Mercury*, 21 April, 3 March 1838.
24. *Leeds Intelligencer*, 26 February 1842.
25. Ivy Pinchbeck, *Women Workers and the Industrial Revolution, 1750 – 1850* (London, 1969 edn), pp. 1 – 5.
26. Eric Richards, 'Women in the British Economy since about 1700: an interpretation', *History*, vol. 59, no. 195 (1974).
27. Thompson, *The Making*, p. 341.
28. Pinchbeck, *Women Workers*, pp. 162 – 5; Duncan Bythell, *The Sweated Trades; Outwork in Nineteenth Century Britain* (London, 1978), pp. 40 – 1.
29. Pinchbeck, *Women Workers*, p. 164.
30. Ibid., p. 117.
31. Bythell, *The Sweated Trades*, pp. 32 – 3.
32. Richards, 'Women in the British Economy'.

33. Ibid.

34. Bythell, *The Sweated Trades*, pp. 75 – 6, 144 – 5, 149.

35. Ibid., p. 131.

36. Richards, 'Women in the British Economy'.

37. Carol Edyth Morgan, 'Working Class Women and Social Movements of Nineteenth Century England', PhD thesis, University of Iowa, 1979, pp. 201 – 2.

38. B. Disraeli, *Sybil* (1954 edn), Book III, Chapter 4.

39. Eve Hostettler, 'Women's Work in the Nineteenth Century Countryside', *Society for the Study of Labour History*, no. 33 (Autumn 1976).

40. Pinchbeck, *Women Workers*, p. 307; J. Saville (ed.), *Working Conditions in the Victorian Age* (Westmead, 1973), p. 174.

41. H. Martineau, 'Female Industry', *Edinburgh Review*, no. 109 (1859), pp. 293 – 336.

42. W. Hasbach, *A History of the English Agricultural Labourer* (London, 1908), p. 230.

43. M. Ramelson, *The Petticoat Rebellion* (London, 1967), p. 25.

44. Hugh Miller, quoted by Eric Richards, 'Women in the British Economy'.

45. Ibid.; Pinchbeck, *Women Workers*, p. 110.

46. Thompson, *The Making*, p. 259; Richards, 'Women in the British Economy'.

47. Ibid.

48. Neale, *Class and Ideology*, p. 148; Harold Perkin, *The Origins of Modern English Society, 1780 – 1880* (London, 1972 edn), p. 157.

49. Pinchbeck, *Women Workers*, p. 307.

50. R. M. Hartwell, *The Industrial Revolution and Economic Growth* (London, 1971), p. 96; Perkin, *The Origins*, pp. 157 – 8.

51. Rhodes Boyson, 'Industrialisation and the Life of the Lancashire Factory Worker', cited by Richards, 'Women in the British Economy'.

52. Neale, *Class and Ideology*, p. 149.

53. Foster, *Class Struggle*, p. 96.

54. Thompson, *The Making*, p. 452.

55. Neale, *Class and Ideology*, p. 148.

56. Thompson, *The Making*, pp. 453 – 4.

57. Bythell, *The Sweated Trades*, p. 220.

58. Cited by Perkin, *The Origins*, p. 157.

59. W. Felkin, *A History of the Machine Wrought Hosiery and Lace Manufactures* (1967 edn), p. 459.

60. E. Baines, *History of the Cotton Manufacture in Great Britain* (1966 edn), p. 486.

61. *English Chartist Circular*, vol. 1, no. 8 (March 1841).

62. P. Branca, *Silent Sisterhood* (London, 1975), p. 54; L. Davidoff, 'Mastered for Life: Servant and Wife in Victorian and Edwardian England', *Journal of Social History*, vol. 7, no. 4 (1974).

63. E. J. Hobsbawm, *Labouring Men* (London, 1976 edn), p. 116.

64. Lewenhak, *Women and Trade Unions*, p. 41.

65. Martineau, 'Female Industry'; P. Gaskell, *Artisans and Machinery* (London, 1968 edn), p. 87.

66. *Poor Man's Guardian*, 10 October 1835.

67. Morgan, 'Working Class Women', p. 231 *et passim*; A. V. John, 'Colliery Legislation and its Consequences: 1842 and the Women Miners of Lancashire', *Bulletin of the John Rylands University Library*, vol. 61 (1978 – 9).

68. Martineau, 'Female Industry'.

69. See, for example, Rudé, *Crowd in History*, pp. 37 – 8; J. Stevenson, 'Food Riots in England, 1792 – 1818' in R. Quinault and J. Stevenson (eds.), *Popular*

Protest and Public Order (London, 1974); Alan Booth, 'Food Riots in the North West of England, 1790 – 1801', *Past and Present*, no. 77 (1977).

Chapter 2

1. E.g. K. J. Logue, *Popular Disturbances in Scotland, 1780 – 1815* (Edinburgh, 1979), p. 199.
2. Of particular importance have been E. P. Thompson, 'The Moral Economy of the English Crowd in the Eighteenth Century', *Past and Present*, no. 50 (1971) and J. Stevenson, 'Food Riots in England, 1792 – 1818' in R. Quinault and J. Stevenson (eds.), *Popular Protest and Public Order* (London, 1974).
3. Stevenson, 'Food Riots in England', pp. 45 – 6.
4. A. Booth, 'Food Riots in the North West of England, 1790 – 1801', *Past and Present*, no. 77 (1977).
5. D. J. V. Jones, *Before Rebecca; Popular Protests in Wales, 1793 – 1835* (London, 1973), p. 199.
6. *The Times*, 23 November 1830.
7. Thompson, 'The Moral Economy'.
8. Cited by Stevenson, 'Food Riots in England', p. 49.
9. Jones, *Before Rebecca*, p. 33.
10. Logue, *Popular Disturbances*, p. 199.
11. Stevenson, 'Food Riots in England', pp. 57, 61.
12. Logue, *Popular Disturbances*, p. 36.
13. *Manchester Mercury*, 21 April 1812.
14. *Leeds Mercury*, 27 August, 1812.
15. J. F. Sutton (ed.), *Nottingham Date Book* (London, 1852), pp. 301 – 2; *Leeds Mercury*, 27 August 1812.
16. *Leeds Mercury*, 27 June 1812.
17. A. J. Peacock, *Bread or Blood* (London, 1965), pp. 79, 104 – 5.
18. Logue, *Popular Disturbances*, p. 199.
19. Jones, *Before Rebecca*, pp. 22 – 3.
20. *The Times*, 30 October 1800.
21. *Northern Star*, 11 May 1839.
22. Booth, 'Food Riots in the North West of England'.
23. Thompson, 'The Moral Economy'.
24. *The Times*, 9 May 1800.
25. *The Times*, 1, 15 and 13 May 1800.
26. *The Times*, 12 and 13 September 1800.
27. *Leeds Mercury*, 18 April 1812.
28. Logue, *Popular Disturbances*, p. 199.
29. *The Times*, 20 September 1800.
30. Thompson, 'The Moral Economy'.
31, Jane Humphries, 'The Working Class Family, Women's Liberation and Class Struggle: the Case of Nineteenth Century British History', *Review of Radical Political Economics*, vol. 9, no. 3 (1977).
32. O. Hufton, 'Women in Revolution', *Past and Present*, no. 53 (1971), pp. 94 – 5.
33. Sutton, *Nottingham Date Book*, p. 247.
34. Logue, *Popular Disturbances*, p. 195.
35. Sutton, *Nottingham Date Book*, p. 247; *The Times*, 3 October 1800.
36. *The Times*, 1 September 1800.
37. Leeds Mercury, 27 August 1812.
38. *The Times*, 19 September 1800.

39. *Manchester Mercury*, 21 April 1812; Stevenson, 'Food Riots in England', p. 58.

40. Stevenson, 'Food Riots in England', p. 58.

41. *The Times*, 19 and 21 September 1800.

42. *The Times*, 12 September 1800.

43. *The Times*, 24 April 1812.

44. Peacock, *Bread or Blood*, pp. 90, 105.

45. Sutton, *Nottingham Date Book*, p. 247.

46. Jones, *Before Rebecca*, p. 26.

47. *The Times*, 23 April 1812.

48. T.S. 11/980, 3581.

49. Stevenson, 'Food Riots in England', pp. 57, 60.

50. *The Times*, 1 November 1800.

51. Stevenson, 'Food Riots in England', p. 45.

52. *Leeds Mercury*, 13 August 1812.

53. Logue, *Popular Disturbances*, p. 36.

54. *The Times*, 23 November 1830.

55. *The Times*, 11 April 1812.

56. *The Times*, 5 September 1800.

57. *The Times*, 1, 9 and 12 September, 1 October 1800.

58. *The Times*, 11 April 1812.

59. *The Times*, 24 April 1812, 21 September 1800.

60. *The Times*, 1 November 1800.

61. *The Times*, 5 September 1800.

62. *The Times*, 21 September 1800.

63. Sutton, *Nottingham Date Book*, pp. 301 – 2.

64. Thompson, 'The Moral Economy'.

65. Stevenson, 'Food Riots in England', pp. 61 – 2.

66. *Leeds Mercury*, 13 August 1812.

67. *Northern Star*, 18 August 1838.

68. Stevenson, 'Food Riots in England', p. 61.

69. *The Times*, 19 September 1800.

70. E.g. G. F. E. Rudé, *The Crowd in History: a Study of Popular Disturbances in France and England, 1730 – 1848* (New York, 1964), p. 205.

71. *Manchester Guardian*, 10 August 1842.

72. Logue, *Popular Disturbances*, p. 195.

73. *The Times*, 23 November 1830.

74. *Political Register*, 25 April 1812.

75. H.O. 52/1, Letter fron Shropshire, 16 November 1820.

76. Logue, *Popular Disturbances*, p. 199.

77. Sutton, *Nottingham Date Book*, p. 221.

78. *The Times*, 5 September 1800.

79. *The Times*, 5 May 1800.

80. *The Times*, 30 August 1800.

81. *The Times*, 12 September 1800.

82. *The Times*, 17 September 1800.

83. *The Times*, 21 April 1812.

84. *The Times*, 19 and 24 April 1812.

85. Booth, 'Food Riots in the North West of England'; *The Times*, 15 April 1800.

86. Jones, *Before Rebecca*, p. 34.

87. *The Times*, 13 October 1800.

88. Ibid.

89. *Leeds Mercury*, 25 July 1812.

90. *Leeds Mercury*, 27 June 1812.
91. T.S. 11/980, 3581; *Manchester Mercury*, 26 May 1812.
92. T.S. 11/980, 3582.
93. Leeds Mercury, 6 June 1812.
94. Peacock, *Bread or Blood*, p. 177.
95. Booth, 'Food Riots in the North West of England'.
96. Stevenson, 'Food Riots in England', pp. 63, 67.
97. L. A. Tilly, 'The Food Riot as a Form of Political Conflict in France', *Journal of Interdisciplinary History*, vol. II, no. 1 (1971).
98. *Manchester Guardian*, 5 December 1838.
99. Stevenson, 'Food Riots in England', p. 64.

Chapter 3

1. *Leeds Mercury*, 25 April, 9 May; *Manchester Mercury*, 21 and 28 April 1812.
2. T.S. 11/980, 3582.
3. T.S. 11/980, 3580.
4. *Leeds Mercury*, 30 May 1812.
5. J. L. and B. Hammond, *The Skilled Labourer* (London, 1919), pp. 54 – 5.
6. *Manchester Guardian*, 29 April 1826.
7. *Manchester Guardian*, 26 August 1826.
8. H.O. 52/5, County returns, 1807 – 21, for political and seditious libel.
9. Frank Peel, *The Risings of the Luddites* (Heckmondwike, 1880).
10. A. J. Peacock, *Bread or Blood* (London, 1965), p. 76.
11. E. J. Hobsbawm and G. F. E. Rudé, *Captain Swing* (London, 1969), p. 246.
12. Ibid., pp. 246 – 9; *The Times*, 16 November 1830.
13. H.O. 52/7, list of prisoners in Gloucester gaol, 1830.
14. Hobsbawm and Rudé, *Captain Swing*, p. 249.
15. H.O. 52/6, T. Westell to H.O., Hungerford, 22 November 1830.
16. H.O. 52/7, *Hampshire Chronicle and Southampton Courier*, 29 November 1830.
17. D. J. V. Jones, *Before Rebecca; Popular Protests in Wales, 1793 – 1835* (London, 1973), p. 45.
18. Ibid., pp. 48, 66, 202.
19. Peacock, *Bread or Blood*, p. 20.
20. Letter from Sir Robert Munro of Fowlis, Cromartie Papers, XIII, 26. We should like to thank Monica Clough of Dunblane for this reference.
21. K. J. Logue, *Popular Disturbances in Scotland, 1780 – 1815* (Edinburgh, 1979), p. 200.
22. Eric Richards, 'Patterns of Highland Discontent, 1790 – 1860' in R. Quinault and J. Stevenson (eds.), *Popular Protest and Public Order* (London, 1974), p. 106.
23. J. Prebble, *The Highland Clearances* (Harmondsworth, 1963 edn), p. 128.
24. A. Mackenzie, *The History of the Highland Clearances* (Glasgow, 1964 edn), pp. 21, 256.
25. Ibid., p. 139.
26. Ibid., p. 144.
27. Richards, 'Patterns of Highland Discontent', p. 101.
28. Prebble, *The Highland Clearances*, pp. 230, 234.
29. Ibid.
30. Ibid., p. 236.
31. Mackenzie, *Highland Clearances*, p. 39.
32. *The Black Dwarf*, 15 March 1820.

33. Quoted by Richards, 'Patterns of Highland Discontent', p. 107.
34. Prebble, *The Highland Clearances*, p. 128.
35. Quoted, for example, by E. P. Thompson, 'The Moral Economy of the English Crowd in the Eighteenth Century', *Past and Present*, no. 50 (1971).
36. Jones, *Before Rebecca*, p. 34.
37. Hammonds, *The Skilled Labourer*, p. 296.
38. Discussed in *Political Register*, 23 August 1834.
39. *Poor Man's Guardian*, 24 May 1834.
40. *Northern Star*, 17 February 1838.
41. M. E. Rose, 'The Anti-Poor Law Agitation' in J. T. Ward (ed.), *Popular Movements, 1830 – 1850* (London, 1970), p. 88.
42. Ibid.; *Northern Star*, 3 March 1838.
43. *Northern Star*, 13 January 1838.
44. *Northern Star*, 25 August 1838; *Leeds Mercury*, 25 August 1838.
45. *Manchester Guardian*, 21 and 24 November 1838.
46. *Northern Star*, 3 November 1838.
47. *The Times*, 22 June and 7 July 1843.
48. *Leeds Mercury*, 1 September 1838.
49. *Leeds Intelligencer*, 30 January and 17 April 1838.
50. *Northern Star*, 10 and 17 February 1838.
51. *Northern Star*, 3 February 1838.
52. *Northern Star*, 27 October 1838.
53. Ibid.
54. *Northern Star*, 22 December 1838.
55. *Northern Star*, 17 February 1838.
56. *Northern Star*, 10 February 1838.
57. *Northern Star*, 17 February 1838.
58. *Northern Star*, 21 April 1838.
59. *Northern Star*, 17 February 1838.

Chapter 4

1. E. P. Thompson, *The Making of the English Working Class* (London, 1968 edn), p. 461.
2. Sheila Lewenhak, *Women and Trade Unions* (London, 1977), p. 21.
3. Ibid., pp. 19 – 20.
4. *Northern Star*, 6 April 1839.
5. *Northern Star*, 10 March 1838.
6. Cited by W. F. Neff, *Victorian Working Women* (London, 1929), p. 35.
7. A. Ure, *The Philosophy of Manufactures* (1835) (1967 edn), p. 23.
8. Sheila Lewenhak, *Women and Work* (Glasgow, 1980), pp. 152 – 3.
9. John Foster, *Class Struggle and the Industrial Revolution* (London, 1974), p. 94.
10. *Report of Select Committee on Combinations, 1837 – 8*, Appendix 2, p. 286.
11. E. P. Thompson, *The Making of the English Working Class* (London, 1968 edn), p. 594.
12. Hamish Fraser, 'Trade Unionism' in J. T. Ward (ed.), *Popular Movements, 1830 – 1850* (London, 1970), pp. 96 – 7.
13. Cited by C. E. Morgan, 'Working Class Women and Social Movements of Nineteenth Century England', PhD thesis, University of Iowa, 1979, pp. 201 – 2.
14. Fraser, 'Trade Unionism', p. 96.
15. Lewenhak, *Women and Work*, pp. 153, 159.

16. Ibid., p. 152.

17. H.O. 42/117, Newcastle to H.O., 16 November, 1811; *Parliamentary Debates*, vol. 57, 967, 26 February 1812.

18. J. L. and B. Hammond, *The Skilled Labourer* (London, 1919), p. 263.

19. Kate Purcell in Sandra Burman (ed.), *Fit Work for Women* (London, 1979), p. 130.

20. *Poor Man's Guardian*, 7 December 1833; 31 May 1834.

21. *The Times*, 29 December 1800.

22. Neff, *Victorian Working Women*, p. 34.

23. A. Aspinall, *The Early English Trade Unions* (London, 1949), p. 390.

24. *Report of Select Committee on Combinations, 1837 – 8*, Appendix 2, p. 286.

25. Ibid., pp. 285, 290.

26. Lewenhak, *Women and Trade Unions*, p. 26.

27. Aspinall, *Early English Trade Unions*, p. 107.

28. Barbara Drake, *Women in Trade Unions* (London, 1921), p. 4.

29. Morgan, 'Working Class Women', pp. 165 – 6.

30. Sheila Rowbotham, *Hidden from History* (London, 1973), p. 32.

31. Lewenhak, *Women and Work*, p. 177,

32. Lewenhak, *Women and Trade Unions*, p. 53.

33. Ibid., pp. 32, 42.

34. *Poor Man's Guardian*, 10 October 1835.

35. *Chartist Circular*, 16 October 1841.

36. Lewenhak, *Women and Trade Unions*, p. 13.

37. Lewenhak, *Women and Work*, p. 176.

38. Aspinall, *Early English Trade Unions*, p. 117.

39. Ivy Pinchbeck, *Women Workers and the Industrial Revolution, 1750 – 1850* (London, 1969 edn), p. 213; Lewenhak, *Women and Trade Unions*, p. 49.

40. Lewenhak, *Women and Work*, p. 176.

41. *The Times*, 25 June 1808.

42. Morgan, 'Working Class Women', p. 78.

43. J.Vaux, 'Women Workers and Trade Unions in Nineteenth Century Britain', *Hecate*, vol. 4 (1978), p. 62.

44. Morgan, 'Working Class Women', pp. 81 – 3.

45. Drake, *Women in Trade Unions*, p. 5.

46. Morgan, 'Working Class Women', p. 307.

47. Ibid., p. 216; Lewenhak, *Women and Trade Unions*, pp. 37 – 43.

48. *Pioneer*, 8 March 1834, cited in P. Hollis (ed.), *Class and Conflict in Nineteenth Century England, 1815 – 1850* (London, 1973), p. 176.

49. Morgan, 'Working Class Women', pp. 195 – 6.

50. Ibid., pp. 207 – 10.

51. Ibid., pp. 215 – 16.

52. Ibid., pp. 205 – 6.

53. Ibid., pp. 204 – 5.

54. *Poor Man's Guardian*, 16 March 1833.

55. *Poor Man's Guardian*, 22 February 1834.

56. Lewenhak, *Women and Trade Unions*, p. 46.

57. *Leeds Mercury*, 4 February 1832.

58. Lewenhak, *Women and Trade Unions*, p. 33.

59. Ibid., p. 36.

60. *Northern Star*, 28 July 1838.

61. *Northern Star*, 16 June 1838.

62. *Northern Star*, 8 December 1838.

63. Morgan, 'Working Class Women', pp. 222 – 6.

64. Ibid., p. 283; Foster, *Class Struggle*, p. 230.

65. *Northern Star*, 2 and 9 May, 13 June 1840.

66. Morgan, 'Working Class Women', pp. 293 – 4.

67. *Poor Man's Guardian*, 25 October 1834; Lewenhak, *Women and Trade Unions*, p. 37.

68. *Report of the Proceedings of the Public Meeting held on Nottingham Forest, 31st March, on the Six Members of the Trade Union at Dorchester* (Nottingham, 1834).

69. S. H. Kydd, *The History of the Factory Movement* (London, 1967 edn), p. 235.

70. Morgan, 'Working Class Women', pp. 133 – 40.

71. Pinchbeck, *Women Workers and the Industrial Revolution*, p. 199.

72. Morgan, 'Working Class Women', pp. 241 – 8.

73. Ibid., pp. 268 – 9.

74. Angela V. John, 'Colliery Legislation and its Consequences: 1842 and the Women Miners of Lancashire', *Bulletin of the John Rylands Library*, vol. 61 (1978 – 9).

75. D. J. V. Jones, *Before Rebecca: Popular Protests in Wales, 1793 – 1835* (London, 1973), p. 78.

76. J. F. Sutton (ed.), *Nottingham Date Book* (London, 1852), pp. 352 – 3.

77. Ibid., p. 454.

78. *Manchester Guardian*, 10 August 1842; *Leeds Intelligencer*, 13 August 1842.

79. *Manchester Guardian*, 14 August 1842.

80. *Manchester Guardian*, 17 August 1842.

81. *Manchester Guardian*, 14 August 1842; *Northern Star*, 13 August 1842.

82. *Manchester Guardian*, 17 August 1842.

83. *Manchester Guardian*, 24 August, 1842.

84. *Leeds Intelligencer*, 20 August 1842.

85. *Manchester Guardian*, 10 August 1842.

86. *Nottingham Review*, 26 August, 1842.

87. *Nottingham Review*, 2 September 1842.

88. *Manchester Guardian*, 17 August 1842.

89. Ibid.

90. *Leeds Intelligencer*, 20 August 1842.

91. *Nottingham Review*, 26 August 1842.

92. *Manchester Guardian*, 20 August 1842; *Leeds Intelligencer*, 20 August 1842.

93. *Leeds Intelligencer*, 27 August 1842.

94. *Northern Star*, 20 August 1842.

95. *Leeds Intelligencer*, 20 August 1842.

96. *Leeds Intelligencer*, 13 August 1842.

97. *Manchester Guardian*, 13 August 1842.

98. *Manchester Guardian*, 17 August 1842.

99. *Manchester Guardian*, 12 October 1842; *Leeds Intelligencer*, 22 October 1842.

100. Hammonds, *The Skilled Labourer*, p. 42.

101. Drake, *Women in Trade Unions*, pp. 6 – 7.

102. Quoted by Lewenhak, *Women and Trade Unions*, p. 42.

Chapter 5

1. Gwyn Williams, *Artisans and Sans-Culottes* (London, 1969), p. 100.

2. K. J. Logue, *Popular Disturbances in Scotland, 1780 – 1815* (Edinburgh, 1979), pp. 106, 121 – 5, 201.

3. *Leeds Mercury*, 28 March 1812.

4. M. I. Thomis and P. Holt, *Threats of Revolution in Britain* (London, 1977), p. 25.

5. S. Bamford, *Passages in the Life of a Radical* (1967 edn), p. 13.

6. Ibid., p. 123.

7. E. P. Thompson, *The Making of the English Working Class* (London, 1968 edn), p. 454.

8. *The Black Dwarf*, 26 February 1817.

9. *The Black Dwarf*, 19 August 1818.

10. *The Black Dwarf*, 9 September 1818.

11. Ibid.

12. Ibid.

13. *The Black Dwarf*, 7 October and 4 November 1818.

14. *The Black Dwarf*, 30 September 1818.

15. *The Black Dwarf*, 16 September 1818.

16. Ibid.

17. *The Black Dwarf*, 4 November 1818.

18. *Annual Register*, 1819. E. P. Thompson, R. S. Neale and Sheila Rowbotham place the first female reform societies in the years 1817 – 18.

19. *Leeds Mercury*, 3 July 1819.

20. *Leeds Mercury*, 17 July 1819.

21. *Manchester Observer*, 10 July 1819.

22. *Manchester Observer*, 17 July 1819.

23. *Leeds Mercury*, 31 July 1819.

24. Ibid.

25. *Leeds Mercury*, 7 August 1819; *Manchester Observer*, 10 July 1819.

26. *Manchester Observer*, 17 July 1819; *The Black Dwarf*, 28 July 1819.

27. *Manchester Chronicle*, 21 August 1819; *Leeds Mercury*, 9 and 23 October 1819.

28. *Manchester Observer*, 17 July 1819; C. E. Morgan, 'Working Class Women and Social Movements of Nineteenth Century England', PhD thesis, University of Iowa, 1979, p. 97.

29. *The Black Dwarf*, 24 November 1819.

30. *Political Register*, 23 October 1819.

31. Ibid.

32. *Manchester Observer*, 31 July 1819.

33. Morgan, 'Working Class Women', p. 89.

34. *Political Register*, 29 December 1819.

35. *Manchester Observer*, 10 July 1819.

36. *Leeds Mercury*, 7 August 1819.

37. *Political Register*, 23 October 1819.

38. *The Black Dwarf*, 10 May 1820.

39. *Manchester Chronicle*, 10 July 1819.

40. *Manchester Chronicle*, 17 July and 14 August 1819.

41. Ibid.

42. *The Black Dwarf*, 24 November 1819; Iain McCalman, 'Females, Feminism, and Free Love, in an Early Nineteenth Century Radical Movement', *Labour History*, no. 38 (1980).

43. *Manchester Observer*, 17 July 1819; *Political Register*, 23 October 1819.

44. Ibid.

45. *The Black Dwarf*, 9 September 1818.

46. *The Black Dwarf*, 14 July 1819.

47. *The Black Dwarf*, 29 September 1819.

48. *The Black Dwarf*, 7 October 1818.

49. *Political Register*, 29 December 1819.

50. *The Black Dwarf*, 10 May 1820.

51. *The Black Dwarf*, 24 November 1819.

52. McCalman, 'Females, Feminism, and Free Love'.

53. Quoted by R. Walmsley, *Peterloo: the Case Reopened* (Manchester, 1969), p. 151.

54. Donald Read, *Peterloo: the Massacre and its Background* (Manchester, 1958), p. 130.

55. Bamford, *Passages*, p. 147.

56. *Leeds Mercury*, 21 August 1819.

57. *Leeds Mercury*, 28 August 1819.

58. Read, *Peterloo*, p. 131.

59. Morgan, 'Working Class Women', p. 98.

60. Bamford, *Passages*, p. 152.

61. *Manchester Observer*, 21 August 1819.

62. *Nottingham Review*, 24 September 1819.

63. Bamford, *Passages*, p. 154.

64. H.O. 52/2, County returns of prosecutions for political and seditious libel, 1807 – 21, *The Black Dwarf*, 2 February 1820.

65. Patricia Hollis, Introduction to reprint of *Poor Man's Guardian, 1831 – 5* (New York, 1969), p. xxvi.

66. Bamford, *Passages*, p. 238.

67. *Nottingham Review*, 10 September 1819.

68. *The Black Dwarf*, 13 November 1822.

69. McCalman, 'Females, Feminism, and Free Love'.

70. *The Black Dwarf*, 24 January 1821.

71. Ibid.

72. H.O. 52/1, Town Clerk of Dover to H.O., 7, 30 July 1820.

73. H.O. 52/1, Mayor of Leeds to H.O., 5 September 1820.

74. McCalman, 'Females, Feminism, and Free Love'.

75. Thompson, *The Making of the English Working Class*, pp. 802 – 3.

76. H.O. 52/8, Gorst Birchall to H.O., Preston, 27 December 1830.

77. *Poor Man's Guardian*, 21 January 1832.

78. *Poor Man's Guardian*, 27 July 1833.

79. *Political Register*, 6 February 1830.

80. *Poor Man's Guardian*, 29 October 1831.

81. D. J. V. Jones, *Before Rebecca; Popular Protests in Wales, 1793 – 1835* (London, 1973), p. 128.

82. Ibid., pp. 143, 146; Gwyn Williams, *The Merthyr Rising of 1831* (London, 1978), pp. 125, 171 – 2.

83. John Wigley, *Nottingham and the Reform Bill Riots of 1831* (Transactions of the Thoroton Society, 1973).

84. *Leeds Mercury*, 5 November 1831.

85. *Manchester Courier*, 12 November 1831.

86. *Poor Man's Guardian*, 21 July 1832.

87. *Poor Man's Guardian*, 15 September 1832.

88. *Poor Man's Guardian*, 26 May 1832.

89. John Foster, *Class Struggle and the Industrial Revolution* (London, 1974), p. 52.

90. *Poor Man's Guardian*, 26 May 1832.

91. *Poor Man's Guardian*, 21 January 1831.

92. *Poor Man's Guardian*, 14 September 1833.

93. *Poor Man's Guardian*, 21 July 1832.

94. *Poor Man's Guardian*, 4 August 1832.

95. Ibid.

96. *Poor Man's Guardian*, 8 December 1832.
97. *Poor Man's Guardian*, 6 October 1832.
98. *Poor Man's Guardian*, 29 December 1832.
99. *Poor Man's Guardian*, 6 July 1833.
100. *Poor Man's Guardian*, 23 March 1833.
101. *Poor Man's Guardian*, 21 July 1832.
102. *Poor Man's Guardian*, 17 May 1834.
103. McCalman, 'Females, Feminism, and Free Love'.
104. *Manchester Courier*, 30 July 1831.
105. *The Black Dwarf*, 17 January 1821.
106. Morgan, 'Working Class Women', pp. 175 – 7.
107. Ibid. pp. 181 – 5.
108. *The Black Dwarf*, 4 November 1818.

Chapter 6

1. *Northern Star*, 25 May 1839.
2. *Northern Star*, 9 February 1839.
3. *Northern Star*, 11 May 1839.
4. *Northern Star*, 12 October 1839.
5. *Northern Star*, 4 May 1839.
6. *Northern Star*, 9 February 1839.
7. *Northern Star*, 22 June 1839.
8. *Northern Star*, 4 June 1842.
9. *Northern Star*, 10 December 1842.
10. *Northern Star*, 3 August 1839.
11. Harold Perkin, *The Origins of Modern English Society, 1780 – 1880* (London, 1972 edn), p. 396.
12. *Northern Star*, 2 February 1839.
13. Ibid.
14. *Northern Star*, 4 May 1839.
15. *Northern Star*, 12 January and 15 June 1839.
16. *Northern Star*, 2 July 1842.
17. *Northern Star*, 25 August 1838.
18. *Northern Star*, 5 January and 27 April 1839.
19. *Northern Star*, 13 October 1838.
20. *Northern Star*, 9 November 1839.
21. *Northern Star*, 26 January and 13 July 1839.
22. *Northern Star*, 18 May 1839.
23. *Northern Star*, 2 February and 18 May 1839.
24. *Northern Star*, 27 October 1838.
25. *Northern Star*, 10 November 1838.
26. *English Chartist Circular*, vol. 1, p. 1.
27. *English Chartist Circular*, vol. 1, p. 19.
28. *English Chartist Circular*, vol. 1, p. 16.
29. *Northern Star*, 24 March 1838.
30. *Northern Star*, 7 December 1839.
31. *English Chartist Circular*, vol. 2, p. 64.
32. *Northern Star*, 16 November 1839.
33. *Northern Star*, 25 May 1839; *English Chartist Circular*, vol. 1, p. 22.
34. *Northern Star*, 29 June 1839.
35. *English Chartist Circular*, vol. 1, p. 16.

36. *Northern Star*, 11 May 1839.
37. *Northern Star*, 5 May 1838.
38. David Jones, *Chartism and the Chartists* (London, 1975), p. 24.
39. *Northern Star*, 8 September 1838.
40. Jones, *Chartism*, p. 182.
41. *Northern Star*, 10 September 1842.
42. *Northern Star*, 10 February 1838.
43. *Northern Star*, 1 June 1839; 12 September 1840.
44. W. Lovett, *Life and Struggles of William Lovett* (1876) (London, 1967 edn), p. 174.
45. *Northern Star*, 2 February 1839; B. Disraeli, *Sybil*, Book VI, Ch. 7.
46. *Northern Star*, 15 June 1839.
47. *Leeds Intelligencer*, 4 September 1841.
48. J. T. Ward, *Chartism* (London, 1973), p. 87.
49. R. B. Pugh, 'Chartism in Somerset and Wiltshire' in A. Briggs (ed.), *Chartist Studies* (London, 1967 edn), p. 207; Jones, *Chartism*, p. 49; Dorothy Thompson, 'Women and Nineteenth Century Radical Politics: a lost dimension' in J. Mitchell and A. Oakley (eds.), *The Rights and Wrongs of Women* (Harmondsworth, 1976), p. 124; *Northern Star*, 29 September and 10 November 1838.
50. *Leeds Intelligencer*, 7 May 1842.
51. *The Times*, 25 and 28 October 1842.
52. *Punch*, XV (1848), p. 3.
53. *Chartist Circular*, 12 September 1840.
54. Disraeli, *Sybil*, Book VI, Ch. 8.
55. *Northern Star*, 26 January 1839.
56. *Northern Star*, 7 March 1840.
57. Jones, *Chartism*, p. 24.
58. *Northern Star*, 8 January 1839; 2 June 1841.
59. Thompson, 'Women and Nineteenth Century Radical Politics', p. 125.
60. Ibid.
61. *Northern Star*, 21 May 1842; C. E. Morgan, 'Working Class Women and Social Movements of Nineteenth Century England', PhD thesis, University of Iowa, 1979, p. 320.
62. Thompson, 'Women and Nineteenth Century Radical Politics', pp. 125, 132.
63. P. W. Slosson, *The Decline of the Chartist Movement* (London, 1967 edn), p. 207.
64. *Northern Star*, 25 August and 8 September 1838.
65. *Northern Star*, 5 May 1838; R. C. Gammage, *History of the Chartist Movement, 1837–54* (London, 1969 edn), p. 82.
66. *Northern Star*, 26 January 1839.
67. Pugh, 'Chartism in Somerset and Wiltshire', p. 177.
68. *Northern Star*, 26 January 1839.
69. *Northern Star*, 18 May 1839; 27 October 1838; 28 December 1839.
70. *Northern Star*, 30 July 1842.
71. *Northern Star*, 17 April 1841.
72. *Northern Star*, 2 January 1841.
73. *Northern Star*, 6 March 1841.
74. *Northern Star*, 29 September 1838.
75. *Northern Star*, 23 November 1839.
76. *Northern Star*, 29 December 1838; 30 March 1839.
77. Morgan, 'Working Class Women', p. 320.
78. *Manchester Guardian*, 26 September 1838.

79. *Manchester Guardian*, 29 May 1839.
80. *Leeds Mercury*, 20 October 1838.
81. *Manchester Guardian*, 21 August 1839.
82. *Northern Star*, 27 October 1838.
83. *Leeds Mercury*, 20 October 1838.
84. *Manchester Courier*, 3 November 1838; *Manchester Guardian*, 21 August 1839.
85. *Manchester Guardian*, 14 November 1838; 27 July 1839.
86. *Northern Star*, 2 January 1841.
87. *Northern Star*, 16 January 1841.
88. *Northern Star*, 15 June 1839; Briggs, *Chartist Studies*, p. 193; *Northern Star*, 1 October and 28 May 1842.
89. Thompson, 'Women and Nineteenth Century Radical Politics', p. 129.
90. Pugh, 'Chartism in Somerset and Wiltshire', p. 186.
91. *Manchester Guardian*, 14 August 1839.
92. Ibid.
93. Disraeli, *Sybil*, Book VI, Ch. 3.
94. *Northern Star*, 9 March 1839.
95. *Northern Star*, 20 April 1839.
96. *Northern Star*, 18 May 1839.
97. *Northern Star*, 13 July 1839.
98. *Northern Star*, 30 July 1842.
99. *Northern Star*, 9 November 1839.
100. *Northern Star*, 13 July 1839; 22 December 1838.
101. *Manchester Guardian*, 3 August 1839; *Northern Star*, 5 October 1839.
102. *Northern Star*, 15 August 1840.
103. *Northern Star*, 2 July 1842.
104. *Northern Star*, 12 October 1839.
105. *Northern Star*, 28 December 1839.
106. *Chartist Circular*, vol. 1, p. 1.
107. *Northern Star*, 13 March 1841.
108. Morgan, 'Working Class Women', p. 323.
109. W. Lovett and J. Collins, *Chartism: a New Organisation of the People (1840)* (Leicester, 1969), pp. 61 – 2.
110. *English Chartist Circular*, vol. 1, p. 13.
111. Thompson, 'Women and Nineteenth Century Radical Politics', p. 131.
112. Morgan, 'Working Class Women', p. 325; *Northern Star*, 8 September 1838.
113. *Northern Star*, 11 May 1839.
114. *Northern Star*, 21 June 1838.
115. R. S. Neale, *Class and Ideology in the Nineteenth Century* (London and Boston, 1972), pp. 147 – 8.
116. N. McCord, *The Anti-Corn Law League, 1836 – 1846* (London, 1958), p. 170.
117. A. Prentice, *History of the Anti-Corn League* (1853) (London, 1968 edn), p. 335.
118. J. W. Croker, *Quarterly Review* (1842 – 3), p. 261.
119. *Leeds Intelligencer*, 15 January 1842.
120. *Leeds Intelligencer*, 10 December 1842.
121. *Northern Star*, 29 April 1848.
122. *Punch*, XV (1848), p. 3.
123. H. Priestley, *Voice of Protest* (London, 1968), p. 255.
124. Thompson, 'Women and Nineteenth Century Radical Politics', pp. 137 – 8.
125. Ibid.; Morgan, 'Working Class Women', p. 345.

Chapter 7

1. Publisher's jacket on M. I. Thomis, *The Luddites* (Newton Abbot, 1970).
2. *The Times*, 17 April 1812; *Political Register*, 25 April 1812.
3. *Manchester Guardian*, 4 December 1830.
4. D. J. V. Jones, *Before Rebecca; Popular Protests in Wales, 1793 – 1835* (London, 1973), p. 61.
5. H.O. 52/1, Augustus Brackenbury to H.O., Cardigan, 12 July 1820.
6. Jones, *Before Rebecca*, p. 61.
7. Ibid., pp. 102, 105; Gwyn Williams, *The Merthyr Rising of 1831* (London, 1978), pp. 29, 71.
8. David Williams, *The Rebecca Riots* (Cardiff, 1955).
9. G. F. E. Rudé, *The Crowd in History: a Study of Popular Disturbances in France and England, 1730 – 1848* (New York, 1964), p. 72.
10. Williams, *The Rebecca Riots*, pp. 188 – 9.
11. Ibid., pp. 191, 199.
12. *The Times*, 30 June and 14 July 1843.
13. *The Times*, 22 June 1843.
14. *The Times*, 14 July 1843.
15. *The Times*, 24 July 1843.
16. Williams, *The Rebecca Riots*, p. 241.
17. *The Times*, 7 July 1843.
18. Douglas Hay *et al.*, *Albion's Fatal Tree* (Harmondsworth, 1977 edn), p. 317.
19. *The Times*, 24 July 1843.
20. *The Times*, 3 July 1843.
21. *Report of Commissioners of Inquiry (South Wales)* and other papers relating to the maintenance of civil order, 1839 – 44 (Irish University Press, Shannon, 1969), q. 5905.
22. Eric Richards, 'Patterns of Highland Discontent, 1790 – 1860' in R. Quinault and J. Stevenson (eds.), *Popular Protest and Public Order* (London, 1974), p. 107.
23. Ibid., *The Black Dwarf*, 15 March 1820.
24. Richards, 'Patterns of Highland Discontent', p. 101.
25. Ibid., p. 107.
26. K. J. Logue, *Popular Disturbances in Scotland, 1780 – 1815* (Edinburgh, 1979), p. 180.
27. *Leeds Mercury*, 15 May 1832.
28. Williams, *The Rebecca Riots*, p. 161.
29. Ibid., p. 207.
30. *The Black Dwarf*, 18 July 1821.

INDEX

agriculture 20, 24, 71
Ancoats, Maria 78
Andrews, J. 43
Anti-Corn Law League 135
anti-Poor Law movement: ideology
63 – 4, 77; organisation and
support 14, 61 – 3, 111, 123 – 4;
reasons for women's involvement
28, 58 – 9; riots 57 – 61; 130
anti-slavery movement 15
arson 9, 10
Ashley, Lord 66 – 7
Ashton 79, 93, 104
Ashton Female Political Union 114,
120
Attwood, T. 126
Australia 10, 15, 56

Bamford, S. 89, 90, 95, 100 – 102
Baptists 143
Barnsley 61 – 2, 83, 115, 127
Barwell, N. 36
Bath 104, 115, 123, 128
Bath Female Radical Association 123
Bentham, J. 110
Benyon, E. 36
Birmingham: Chartist leadership 114,
116, 118, 132; Chartist
organisation and support 119,
124 – 6, 131; occupations of
workforce 19, 68, 74; trade-
unionism 65, 75, 77
Birmingham Female Chartist
Association 119
Birmingham Female Political Union
131
Birmingham Political Union 105 – 6
Blackburn 48, 92, 95, 99, 102, 104
Blackburn Female Reform Society
92, 96, 99, 100
Black Dwarf 90 – 2, 97 – 8, 143
Bolton 43, 82, 104, 128
bonnet-makers 25, 74 – 5, 86
Brackenbury, A. 139
Bradford: anti-Poor Law movement
59, 61; charitable activities 15, 16;
Chartist organisation and support
115, 124 – 36; food-riots 37, 39;
Queen Caroline support 102; trade
unionism 66, 76
Bradford-upon-Avon Patriotic
Association 125
Brady, Mary 135
Brady, Roba 135

Bristol 106, 115, 131
Bristol Female Patriotic Association
113
British and Foreign Bible Society 86
Brooks, Hannah 105
Butterworth, A. 47
Byron, Benjamin 31

Calton Universal Suffrage
Association 120, 131
Carlile, Jane 104
Carlile, Mary 104
Carlile, Richard 104, 107, 110
Carlisle: anti-Poor Law movement
61 – 2; Chartist support 125, 131;
food-riots 36 – 7; 42
Carlisle Female Radical Association
131
Carmarthen 60, 105, 140 – 2
Carney, Jane 85
Carr, Elizabeth 86
Cartwright, John 100
Castlereagh, Viscount 93
Castles the spy 91
Catherall, Ann 56
Celtic Fringes 52, 140
Chartism: activities of women 13, 60,
126 – 32; decline in women's
involvement 136 – 7; inhibitions
and exploitation of women 26, 72,
118 – 22; organisation and support
11, 14, 23, 62, 123 – 6; reasons for
women's involvement 58, 111 – 15,
116 – 18; religious inspiration 16,
115 – 16; women's rights 77,
132 – 5
Cheshire 45, 61, 77
Children's Employment
Commissioners 25
City of London Female Charter
Association 132
Civil liberty 23
Clare, Margaret 36, 85
Close, Rev. Francis 123
clothing trade 19
Cobbett, William 89, 94 – 5, 97 – 8
Cobden, Richard 135
colliers 32, 33
Colne 63, 116, 127
Combe, St Nicholas 60
Combination Laws 65
Communist Manifesto 133
convicts 9, 10, 15
Cookson's factory 77